Praise for *Hope in the Darkness*

"With the first words of the introduction to Hope in the Darkness, Dana Picore had me. Those words dealt with fear—fear by causing harmful reactions and unwarranted fear by causing overreactions. She urges us to broaden our news input and seek wider sources in general, telling us easy does it, slow down, don't jump to judgment—priceless words we all should listen to and heed. Above all, this book is about resisting fears so that they don't control our lives. The many chapters within show us how to interpret threats and respond to them."

—Ed Asner, Emmy Award-winning actor and former president of the Screen Actor's Guild

"In the midst of the incessant barrage of the negative news transmitted over a twenty-four-hour basis by networks interested only in high ratings, this book written by a veteran in law enforcement and psychology reminds of us how important it is to maintain a hopeful attitude about the world and to see things in perspective and not through the lens of sensationalism. I highly recommend you read this book as I have."

—Eric Braeden, Emmy Award-winning actor, received Humanitarian Award from the government of Israel by Ambassador Yuval Rotem

"Dr. Picore, with her years of experience as a police officer and threat assessor, shares her insight and gems of strategies on how to bounce back from adversity and struggles, whether personal or workplace related. She shares real-life stories and guides us to learn from debilitating circumstances. She reminds us that hope is a powerful choice."

—Werner Hellmann, retired captain, NYPD, and a US Marine Corps veteran

"Dr. Picore poignantly illustrates that the H in hope stands for help. She guides you through real-life crisis and interjects resourceful information to help you through what appears to be a mountain of challenges when faced with a traumatic personal event or potential workplace violence. Her ten-point threat assessment model presents a blueprint of resources that can be applied to almost every crisis."

— Art Lopez, Oxnard, CA, retired Chief of Police; retired Deputy Chief, Los Angeles Police

"Dr. Dana Picore, a top successful threat assessor and motivational coach, inspires us to shift focus from dwelling in a disempowered state by harnessing the power of a can-do attitude and the application of common-sense strategies, which she eloquently illustrates in her book Hope in the Darkness. *Her ten-point threat assessment model is riveting. It's a must-read."*

—Stephen A. Smith, American sports television personality and commentator on ESPN's First Take, radio host, journalist, and actor

HOPE

IN THE DARKNESS

DANA PICORE, Ph.D.

THE 10-POINT THREAT ASSESSMENT MODEL

HOPE

IN THE DARKNESS

Advantage®

Published by Advantage, Charleston, South Carolina.
Member of Advantage Media Group.

Printed in the United States of America.

10 9 8 7 6 5 4 3 2 1

ISBN: 978-1-59932-764-8
LCCN: 2017950349

Book design by Megan Elger.

For my grandparents, George and June Gordon,
who were always there for me during turbulent times . . . and to
all the victims of mass shootings and various types of
violence in the United States and internationally.

Contents

Before implementing any workplace violence prevention program at your organization, please consult legal counsel, human resources, and a threat assessment expert.

A WORD FROM THE AUTHOR

I wrote *Hope in the Darkness* to help others, and not until it was complete did I realize how much it was inspired by my childhood. With the knowledge and experience one attains in adulthood and as a business owner, I was able to reflect back on the culmination of events to date and in doing so realized that who I am today has everything to do with how I was raised. You would think with a Ph.D. in psychology that would be obvious, but it is always easier to see in others what you cannot see in yourself. As is often true with those who have achieved success or drive in their fields, mine was not an easy childhood. But those hard times allowed me to reach deep down inside and pull out the best of myself.

I entered this world without a father—abandoned while my mother was giving birth. As a child I contracted a kidney infection and the prescribed medications had severe side effects. Once a skinny little girl, I found myself bloated, appearing heavy set, and as happens so often, it opened the door to incessant teasing and bullying for many years. The depression and isolation one feels at an early age can stay with you for a lifetime. Ironically, the very thing that I was being teased and bullied for drove me to seek solace in food as comfort, which only amplified the issue.

My elementary school years found me dealing with a horrific speech impediment. I saw a speech therapist for years, learning to pronounce words correctly so others could understand what I was saying—yet another hurdle to overcome.

When my mother remarried, she unfortunately did so to a man who was a compulsive gambler and verbally abusive to us both. I found myself increasingly isolated and withdrawn as my world began to cave in around me. It was then I started to understand the word "darkness," and with that word I chose to find another: "hope."

It wasn't obvious to me then, but it was how I found my calling in the world of law enforcement and security.

You see, hope is a necessary ingredient in all aspects of life. It allows us to ground ourselves and know that in the near future it can be better. It tells us not to allow fear to overcome us, because if fear takes over we will never achieve our dreams. We must take control of our lives and lend a helping hand to the person next to us because by helping others we actually help ourselves.

Today, I have a personal trainer, go to the gym, and try to eat healthy. I have a successful business and relationships that build me up, not pull me down. Today, companies call me and ask how to defuse and contain violence and how to move forward in a healthy direction. Hope in the Darkness is a guide toward the positive.

May all of us continue to have hope. I know I do.

www.picoreinternational.com

INTRODUCTION

Hope against Fear

During the 1992 riots following the verdict of Rodney King's trial, I was an officer with the Los Angeles Police Department (LAPD) working the Hollywood division. Fires were blazing everywhere, and business owners were on their rooftops with shotguns protecting their stores from rioters and looters. I was on a large public bus with forty fellow police officers in riot gear.

"I'm scared," a rookie officer whispered to me, so the other guys wouldn't hear.

"Don't worry—we're riding with the best department in the world," I told him. "Everyone here is scared and taking their anger out on each other. But the National Guard is on its way to back us up. You have to understand these are citizens; do your best to handle them one by one. Keep your emotions in check. Here we go!"

Normally upstanding citizens, these people had lost their individuality in the unruly crowd mentality. Perceived injustice is usually the spark. If one burns a car, the others will follow.

Police officers in situations like the one we faced have to use their fear as momentum to act, but they can't let it take over and turn into excessive force.

We are fed a constant diet of fear—on the TV, smartphones, newspapers, and online. We are immersed in a fear-based culture that is amplified by modern technology and a media culture that promotes sensationalism and slants the information they cover to suit their political leanings. Let's face it—how much does watching the news improve your mood or enhance your sense of security? As I write this book, we are in the midst of recurring attacks both on American soil and overseas. Our response as a society is to either tighten our borders or launch preemptive attacks, which, as we have seen in the past, can leave power vacuums, bigger threats, and more fear. How secure do you feel as you read about the growing number of terrorist attacks in the world?

For terrorism to work, it must instill terror. This keeps us from living normally. It keeps us from getting on planes and traveling to foreign destinations. It causes us to isolate ourselves and avoid crowds. It can cause us to react in ways we normally wouldn't. It can cripple us physically and emotionally. It can even undermine the economy and ultimately affect livelihoods much more than the terrorists alone ever could.

If you're feeling a heightened sense of anxiety, you're not alone. The constant barrage of negative news that pervades our world today can cause us to feel helpless, hyper-aroused, overly fearful, or overly protective. Others just shut down, and some become preoccupied with the suffering of the people directly affected, a condition known as "compassion fatigue."

If you're growing weary of the overwhelming number of negative images and reports, if you're starting to feel like the world is truly a violent place, then it's time to put things in perspective. It's time to roll out your most powerful weapon against fear—not just guns, barbed wire, or pepper spray but *hope*.

Thirty years of work in law enforcement, private security, and psychology has shown me up close the power of hope in conquering fear. My interdisciplinary background has taught me that hope comes from empowerment and education. And so, to give you knowledge and power, I wrote this book to help you understand some basic principles about threats. By educating yourself about threatening circumstances and discovering effective and measured solutions, I hope to help you reduce or alleviate fear.

You don't need to stop following the news, either. Just be more discerning and consider the source of your information; so much on traditional media is spun, and so much on social media is not vetted at all. Too much negativity isn't healthy, and it can begin to control your behavior and how you interact with the world. Balance is key. Balance out the negative with positive things in your life. The vast majority of people get their news from similar sources or from within an online group of people who tend to feel and believe similarly. This new trend leaves readers in an information "bubble," subjecting them to viewpoints that only appeal to one's already assumed perspective rather than sharing objective new positions and information that can help them gain fresh insights to be considered. If one can take the time to broaden their "bubbles," it can also help give perspective, understanding, and an overall balance in news consumption.

This is especially important to understand if you're a business owner or leader, as too much negativity can impact the decisions you make in the workplace. Always remember that hope is the best weapon we have against fear.

That's what this book is about: empowering yourself emotionally to keep fear in its place. It's about becoming knowledgeable and understanding the difference between a real and perceived threat so you don't become paranoid. With the information I'm going to share, I want you to attain a certain perspective so fear doesn't affect you psychologically and impact your life or the decisions you make at your organization.

CHAPTER I

A New Perspective

For decades, we have had to deal with mass shootings in public schools, yet most people still send their children to get an education. It seems as though there are too many instances of disgruntled workers killing people at their job sites to keep track anymore, yet people still have to go to work every day. But when a terror attack occurs, it's easy to have a knee-jerk reaction and believe a terrorist is around every corner. That's fear driving the bus.

Everyone wants to feel safe and secure. The key to managing fear and maintaining hope is to keep things in perspective.

According to the *Washington Post*, 130 people died in the attacks in Paris in 2015, but three times that many French citizens died that same day from cancer.[1] The *Daily Mail* reported that thirty-two thousand people were killed by terrorists in 2014, a single-year increase of 80 percent. But the majority of those deaths were in areas of major civil strife. According to the Institute for Economics

1 Andrew Shaver, "You're More Likely to Be Fatally Crushed by Furniture Than Killed by a Terrorist," *The Washington Post,* November 23, 2015, accessed March 22, 2016, www.washingtonpost.com/news/monkey-cage/wp/2015/11/23/youre-more-likely-to-be-fatally-crushed-by-furniture-than-killed-by-a-terrorist/.

and Peace, more than six thousand of the nearly eighteen thousand people killed in 2014 by terrorist attacks were in Iraq alone.[2]

Consider this: as an American, the chances are roughly one in twenty million that you will be killed by a terrorist attack in the US.[3] That means you're more likely to be killed by a random act or a falling object than a terrorist attack.[4] In terms of disease, the Centers for Disease Control reports that you are:

- 35,079 times more likely to die from heart disease
- 33,842 times more likely to die from cancer
- 4,311 times more likely to die from diabetes
- 3,157 times more likely to die from flu or pneumonia
- 4,706 times more likely to drink yourself to death[5]

So why do we still fear harm from others more than anything else? In a society that isn't equipped to take care of every individual, caring for yourself is extremely important, making the fear of others a somewhat natural reaction. Being vigilant of threats is good, but it's also stressful when done hyperactively. Educating yourself about threats can reduce stress by helping you know when to perceive a threat and when not to. Think of it as a kind of preventive maintenance for anyone stressed by violent stories and bad news. You can also reduce stress by limiting your intake of the news media. When fear threatens to take hold, take a deep breath and tell yourself that

---

2 Eva Shield, "What Are Your Chances Of Being Killed In A Terrorist Attack?" *Press for Truth*, March 22, 2105, accessed March 23, 2016, https://pressfortruth.ca/top-stories/what-are-your-chances-being-killed-terrorist-attack/.

3 Richard Barrett, coordinator of the United Nations al Qaeda/Taliban Monitoring Team in *Time*, May 6, 2013, accessed March 23, 2016, http://swampland.time.com/2013/05/06/chances-of-dying-in-a-terrorist-attack-number/.

4 Shield, "What Are Your Chances Of Being Killed In A Terrorist Attack?"

5 National Counterterrorism Center (2011), cited in *WashingtonsBlog*, "What Is the REAL Risk from Terrorism?" June 8, 2015.

it's okay to feel fear, but that fear must not take control. With a little education, fear can actually be a gift. All of our fears, no matter how irrational they may seem to us today, are in some sense survival-based from our primitive lives. It does not always serve us well in modern age, however, it is still important to pay attention to our instinctive cues. Fear is helpful where anxiety is not and can be related to phantom events that often don't happen.

Respect as a Defense

"One L-12, respond to 633 Sixth Street: 415 fight [two men fighting] in the middle of the road. Respond code two high," the precinct's radio crackled.

My partner and I responded to the call. Just twenty-five years old, I had been on the job for two years. My partner wasn't much older. Luckily, defusing explosive situations had always come naturally to me. I had learned to use my own fear to my advantage and take control of the situation. When we arrived, we saw two men fighting in the middle of the street. Undaunted, my partner grabbed one of the suspects, and I grabbed the other and pinned him up against the police unit. I was holding his hands behind his back, but I knew by his resistance that he was much stronger than I was. If he got free, there would be a fight between us, and I was in no doubt about whom the winner would be. Neither additional force nor enforcements were available. I had to think fast.

"Sir, it doesn't have to be this way. I want to help you, and I need you to relax," I said, making sure I sounded assertive and persuasive at once. "The last thing I want is to put a help call out because then there will be twenty cops here to assist me."

I was trained to be cautious in these situations. With all that adrenalin pumping, I had to stay focused or someone could get hurt or killed—including me. I knew never to get cocky or I'd pay for it. Be humble, be thoughtful, educate yourself, and listen to your gut.

Respect can go a long way when dealing with threatening individuals or situations. In this case, I was showing him respect by talking to him in a nondemeaning way, yet making sure he understood the consequences of continued hostility, and this diffused the situation.

"Hey, it's okay. It's a bad day and tomorrow will be better," I said. "It does not have to go down this way. No one has to get hurt. No one here wants to hurt you. Let's take it down a notch and talk about this."

I never used the phrase "calm down," because it has the exact opposite effect—it lights you on fire and not in a good way. Had I screamed at the man or been verbally abusive, the situation would have escalated and I would have undoubtedly had a fight on my hands. Of course, this isn't the appropriate response if someone is very violent or wielding a weapon, but in this situation, it was the best approach.

Arguably, society has become increasingly stressed over the last two decades. Every day, it seems, we're exposed to people—sometimes a great number of people—in a great amount of pain. Witnessing depravity can add to the stresses we experience in a normal day. The barrage of online videos showing atrocities can often show only one perspective in a scenario. The recent uproar regarding bias in the police force and a lack of accountability will only grow if we do not take steps to train "diffusion" rather than escalation. When videos displaying the type of enforcement I'm describing begin to appear in the media, I have no doubt that a greater appreciation will spread for law enforcement, inspiring a change in people's view of not only police but also of how to deal with their own potential threatening scenarios.

Law Enforcement: Under Pressure

It is important to remember that *not* all police are bad. Like any other profession, the vast majority of law enforcement are honest, hardworking men and women with families of their own who are just trying to do the right thing. There is, however, a growing body of evidence showing that law enforcement personnel are at the upper end of the spectrum for occupational stress.[6] They see the real world every day on the job, and they generally see more of the ugly side than the good side of people. When I was working patrol, for example, my partner and I went from one call to another, as is typical. "6 Adam 10 respond to a 415 man in the middle of the street with a knife"; then, "6 Adam 10 respond to a gang fight on Hollywood and Vineland"; "6 Adam 10 Code 37 stolen car"; "6 Adam 8 needs back up." Back-to-back calls can take their toll on anyone, let alone people putting themselves in harm's way, every day, all day. Hollywood, CA, station was a busy site to work, with a vast amount of calls ranging from simple traffic stops to high-risk calls. When you're an officer, you have to remember that even a traffic stop can turn deadly.

An officer's stress can be compounded by the fact that formal training of law enforcement does not necessarily include the most positive or productive coping skills. The message in the typical police training program is: "You're the last line of defense. You're out there to handle it. It's tough, but that's what you get paid for."

To put the problems with this kind of training into perspective, consider it from a non-officer's perspective: A lawsuit was recently filed against a major software corporation arguing that workers who

---

6 Mark Bond, "The Impact of Stress and Fatigue on Law Enforcement Officers and Steps to Control It," accessed April 4, 2017, http://inpublicsafety.com/2014/02/the-impact-of-stress-and-fatigue-on-law-enforcement-officers-and-steps-to-control-it/.

were exposed to a daily barrage of videos to monitor content caused them to suffer from PTSD.[7] You read that correctly, just the videos of the trauma caused PTSD. Now imagine, if you will, that law enforcement officers are routinely exposed to the same situations; however, they are doing it real time, with no pause button, and in person. So if just viewing a pixelated video of these atrocities can induce PTSD in those who view them, imagine the impact on officers who are not just seeing these events in a blurred video but up close and personal on a routine and daily basis.

Training to deal with scenarios is only one portion of the job; learning how to deal with the aftermath and the emotional toll it can have is essential to good leadership moving forward. We need to make sure that the compounded effect doesn't roll over into the next day and the next one after that. This is why proper training cannot be strictly field related. It must also deal with the psychological aspects of the job.

Focusing on de-escalation and prioritization of an event can do a great deal to help officers learn coping skills and, at the same time, can also help repair their image in the public eye. We tend to forget that officers, while sometimes hardened by what they do over time, still experience emotion and have families and loved ones they need to come home to while knowing that they have done their best to protect and serve. A great story of taking a situation, evaluating it for its threat level, and regaining the respect and understanding of a community is the story of Officer White. He became a YouTube sensation when he responded to a disturbance call while on patrol for the Gainesville Police Department.

---

7 Michael Harthorne, "Microsoft made employees watch child porn and murder, lawsuit claims," accessed April 4, 2017, www.usatoday.com/story/news/nation/2017/01/11/microsoft-made-employees-watch-child-porn-and-murder-lawsuit-claims/96439086/?.

"[Can] you believe someone's calling to complain about kids playing basketball in the street?" Officer White asks a boy holding a basketball when he arrived at the scene on the YouTube video. "I don't know who called, but obviously, I ain't got no problem with it." Officer White then grabs the basketball, takes a shot, and misses. "That's a nice hoop," Officer White says.

After playing basketball for a little while with the kids, Officer White heads toward his patrol car. As he does, he asks the boys not to be too loud and tells them to have fun. Before he leaves, he says he'll be back with backup the next day . . . to get another game going. "We're going to let kids be kids," the Gainesville police state in their popular video. "We're going to focus on the ones that commit crimes." Officer White continues to play with the kids on the block to this day.

This kind of positive interaction with the community helps serve not only the public but the officers as well. Building rapport in the community and focusing on real crime can be a win-win for all involved. Could he have cited them for a noise complaint? Sure. Was that the proper move when it was kids playing rather than participating in other potential criminal activities? Absolutely not. Learning to release tension and at the same time receive positive feedback from those in the community can go a long way in helping an officer have a positive outlook, which only helps them do their jobs better. The trickle down is that the community knows they have people they can trust to see a situation and handle it appropriately.

Unfortunately, the light moments on the job can be few and far between. Stressful moments on the job can take their toll, pushing some police officer into a cycle in which images of violence recur and escalate. With each mental representation, imagination, or rehearsal, the officer imagines further potentially devastating outcomes. The officer's mental process might involve something like this: "If the suspect is at the location and has a knife, I could attempt to use my Taser. If that is ineffective, or if he charges me, then I may attempt a retreat. If that fails, then I may have to use deadly force."

Policing is a challenging occupation characterized at the top by a rigid bureaucratic structure; yet from the perspective of the street officer, there is a great deal of discretion and autonomy. Anyone who has been in law enforcement has experienced this on some level in their years on the force but so have security directors, human resources professionals, managers, and organization leaders who feel the pressure to protect others. If you are in one of these roles, then you have a responsibility for others' lives and are trusted by the organization to make the right decisions. It's hard enough to run an organization without having to be constantly vigilant for potential threats, which makes educating yourself and keeping everything in perspective even more important to ensure a balanced, responsible, effective, and healthy sense of preparedness.

Take school violence as an example. Just as it's important to talk to your age-appropriate children about what to do should a threat at school arise, so it is for the workplace as well. Communicating with and educating employees on threats and the appropriate responses just may save their lives.

Unfortunately we see too often how this plays out when preventative steps are not taken. Some years ago in San Francisco, for instance, Gian Luigi Ferri, a fifty-five-year-old failed entrepreneur, entered a building on California Street and took the elevator to the offices of law firm Pettit & Martin on the thirty-fourth floor. He then put on ear protection and used the stairs to work his way down to lower floors as he shot and killed eight people before taking his own life. People in the offices hid in various rooms, but none of the doors had locks on them. Ferri's reason for targeting the firm is unknown, as Pettit & Martin had merely redirected him to alternative legal counsel about some real estate deals in the Midwest in 1981 and had not heard from him in the twelve years after.

Do you have a plan for what you would do should a shooter enter the room? Having such measures in place doesn't mean you're more paranoid today than you were yesterday; it means you're wiser and more prepared. Security audits should and will become an essential tool to many businesses moving forward. Learning from scenarios like this one only helps us assess potential risks. Having a security audit should provide a business with the tools they need to protect themselves and their workers. The necessity of this cannot be understated.

It is similar to insurance. You buy insurance to cover yourself in case of disaster. Even though the likelihood of a disaster is slim, you wouldn't think of cancelling your policy. This is what it means to prepare and empower yourself instead of being anxious and fearful.

I have a number of clients who can attest to this. They operate brick-and-mortar stores in some high-risk areas, such as Compton, Detroit, and Houston. Why? Because that's where their target market is located. Do they operate with a false sense of security? No. They have armed guards and take other necessary precautions to protect their staff and their livelihood. If they let themselves be immobilized by fear, they'd be out of business. Fear doesn't stop any of them—large or small—from doing business and living their life. If there is an incident, I make sure they are prepared for it ahead of time so they can get back up and keep moving forward. That preparation all begins with a model I created as a starting point for dealing with threats, potential or real.

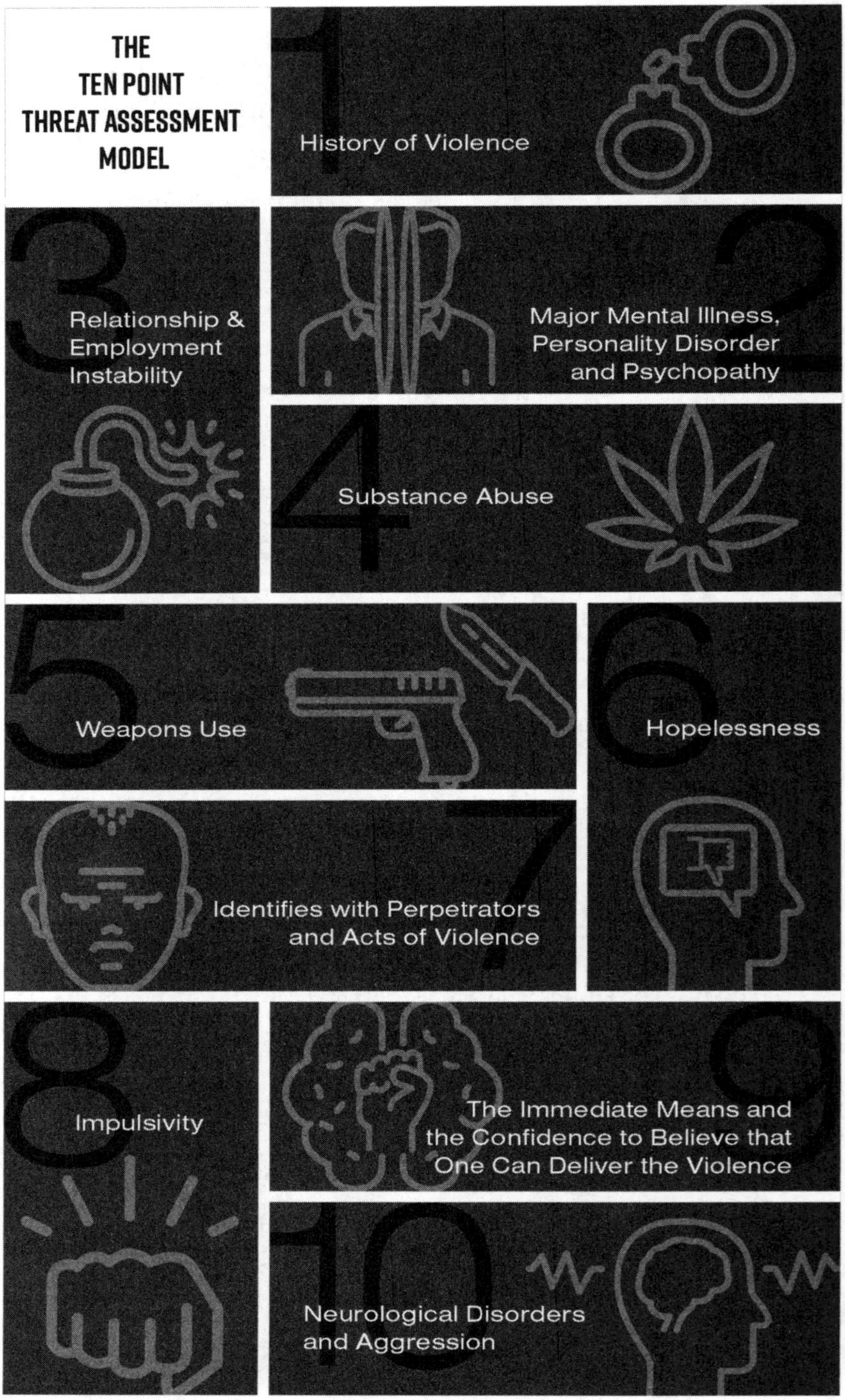

The Ten Point Threat Assessment Model is not a checklist. It is utilized as a guide to assist in the evaluation. Look for positive and negative changes in behavior. © Picore International.

The 10-Point Threat Assessment

Threat assessment and management is an integral part of keeping the fear out of the business of doing your daily business. A threat assessment can help your organization define security risks potentially arising from employees, customers, or visitors. A threat assessment can also help an organization anticipate when violence may be imminent, and it can help reduce factors that can lead to violent acts.

In the chapters that follow, I'll explain my 10-Point Threat Assessment Model. This model can help you to conduct a threat assessment and evaluate the propensity or potentiality of violence. The information in this book can empower you to understand whether a person is a potential threat and then help you decide whether the situation is one you're capable of managing or whether you need a security consultant.

Threat assessment is an art; instead of instantly deploying heavy-handed tactics, although this may be needed on a case-by-case basis, intervention may involve clever, less-invasive tactics to bring about a resolution. As a threat assessment consultant, I work with your organizations' key personnel—human resources, corporate security, legal team, supervisors, and other staff members—and combine both science and instincts when gathering information to fully understand the situation. Utilizing a form of psychological behavioral profiling, questions, and scenario recreation, an assessment is then created to determine how your team will react and handle these types of situations. Most importantly, we can then work with your team to develop the necessary skill set to respond appropriately if the necessity arises.

While the layers and nuances of threats differ, there is fundamental information that everyone should know to be better able to protect their safety and the safety of others. A threat does not necessarily mean there's anything to fear. For example, a person can pose a grave threat without articulating it. "Some people who make threats ultimately pose threats; some people who pose threats never make threats."[8]

What follows is some valuable information that you can use when working with a trained threat assessment expert. It's not intended to be a step-by-step guide to assessing a potential threat yourself. No single point alone can predict violence and not all high-risk cases will have all ten of the threat assessment points. When there are links between one or more of these points, then the threat may be even greater but not always. For example, violence often has a link to intoxication, but just because someone has an issue with drinking doesn't mean they're going to be violent.

In other words, never rely solely on a checklist to conduct a threat assessment. The responsibility for assessing a threat rests with the assessor in the situation; he or she must be aware and observant of significant factors when determining the dangers a person poses. In a business setting and when reporting incidents to authorities, you must take care not to assess a threat in clinical terms, as this can become a liability for your company. Instead, it's best to describe actions or behaviors. For example, people prone to violence often exhibit similar pre-attack behaviors. In cases where people plan some type of targeted violence, there are usually signs. In school violence, there's often an unspoken "code of silence" among students and they don't usually see the larger picture.

We need to identify, assess, and manage the threat but never expect the checklist to provide all the answers. No single check box will be enough to tell us what is motivating a person to be violent. We can prepare for the worst, though, and hope (once again) for the best.

---

8 Joseph A. Davis, *Stalking Crimes and Victim Protection: Prevention, Interventions, Threat Assessment, and Case Management* (Boca Raton, LA: CRC Press, 2001), 508.

Threat assessment is an ever-evolving landscape. They should be designed for the short term, capable of adapting as people's lives, environments, and circumstances change. A person assessed today as nonthreatening, may, six months from now, get a divorce, buy a gun, and start drinking or taking drugs until they are very much a threat to others as well as themselves. A change in a person's behavior is often your first indication that something may need further scrutiny. Knowing that you put a plan like this in place gives you the confidence to be positive and hopeful.

Ultimately, when it comes to assessing threats, it's important to find balance. Too much fear can hobble an organization, while too much hope can place your organization at risk. By arming yourself with information, knowing when to perform an assessment, and then taking measures to protect against potential threats, you can better protect yourself, your family, your staff, and your organization as a whole.

What Can Be Done!

Police and other security professionals should develop a short-term plan to interrupt an actual threat. Long-term plans aim to help the desperate person to move into a hopeful mindset. Unless you are dealing with an enraged individual, such as an active shooter, there are many things you can do to defuse and try to understand the person in front of you. Express understanding, ask questions to discover solutions, and ask about his or her needs. Sometimes aggressive self-defense will be the only response, but if you use respect, empathize, and focus on de-escalating the situation (not curing the person), then your odds of a peaceful resolution will skyrocket.

CHAPTER 2

Fear, Anger, Rage, and a History of Violence

"I can see why employees go postal," Anderson said to me in our first conversation. "I don't agree with it, but I can see why people go nuts. Management pushed them over the edge . . ."

Anderson was a longtime employee of a company that had contacted me for a consult. Over the prior six months, the management team had become increasingly concerned about his emotional outbursts. Anderson had two "demands": (1) change of job classification and (2) transfer out of the facility.

Management had transferred Anderson to another facility, but since then he had once again become angry and wanted to be transferred back to the original facility—a request that was denied.

"I either win or I am leaving on a disability," he said. "I tried to get a transfer out of the shop and I can't even do that."

He was very upset during our conversation because he felt that he deserved to be classified at a higher level than his current class comp rating. I tried on several occasions to move him toward the positive aspects of the company, but I was met with little success. Instead, he discussed his lack of sleep over the job classification that appeared to be consuming his life. I told him that I was worried about his health and that he needed to try to balance his quest for his perceived justice with other leisure activities in his life to ward off some of the stress.

Instead, he asked me, "Do you know how many Americans lost their lives in war?"

"Over one hundred thousand in certain wars."

"They died for a cause that they believed in," he said, barely hearing my response. "If I have a shorter life because of this battle that I believe in, then so be it."

Anderson's anxiety, loss of emotional control, agitation, intense anger, and irritability made me realize that he did not feel safe. In his mind, management was out to get him. His coping skills were not well developed, and quite possibly something had happened to him in his past that kept him stuck in the past. He continued to stew on the negative. When a person says he or she thinks they can hurt others or themselves, my recommendation is very simple: *listen to them.*

Anderson acknowledged that he needed help from the Employee Assistance Program (EAP) to vent in a confidential setting. In addition, he had sought my assistance many times over the past six months to vent his anger and frustration. What he failed to understand, though, was that his continued anger and frustration was fueling him toward full-on rage. This rage could be dangerous for both him and others. When threats are introduced late in the game, they tend to be more concerning than are those observed early on in a threat assessment. Anderson had introduced these threats late in the game. As a self-proclaimed crusader, he'd attached himself to the mission of the class comp pay scales, and it appeared that he was ready to wage a one-man war against his company.

One of the most important factors in determining future violent behavior is past violent behavior. A history of violence is one variable that tips us off to a potential workplace threat.

There is an environmental influence, meaning if you remove the person from the environment they may not be violent in a different environment.

The probability of violence increases in a linear pattern with the number of past violent acts. It is a person who lacks sophisticated reasoning, stabilization, perspective, and emotion to regulate his more primitive fear and aggressive impulses. Psychological scientists who study human behavior agree that past behavior is a useful marker for future behavior but only under certain specific conditions:

- High-frequency habitual behaviors.
- Predictions work best over short time intervals.
- The anticipated situation must be essentially the same as the past situation that activated the behavior.
- The behavior must not have been extinguished by corrective or negative feedback.
- The person must remain essentially unchanged.
- The person must be fairly consistent in his or her behavior.

Once again, one of the best predictors of future behavior is past behavior, let me add that this is only under specific conditions. One of those conditions is high frequency. Habitual behaviors are more predictive than infrequent behaviors, so if someone regularly engages in bar fights or is a known spouse abuser, then that behavior is likely to continue unless something changes in that person's life. However, if someone acted violently in their teens or as a young adult—maybe they got into many fights, for example, or spent more time in bars and ended up in bar fights—that doesn't necessarily mean they're still prone to fistfights when they're in their thirties or forties.

In Anderson's case, however, the company didn't sit idle. Management implemented many intervention strategies to contain Anderson, including six EAP sessions. Ms. Sun, Anderson's manager, met with him several times to hear his frustrations. The company also initiated a leave of absence so he could regroup and gave him strong boundaries for when he returned to work. Anderson was also given the opportunity to use me as a sounding board.

Anderson was classified as a "medium threat" because of his indirect threats, open defiance of the rules, belief that others were conspiring against him, and severe emotional distress. Each category has a set of guidelines that helps determine an individual's level of potential violence. Again, although there are categories that offer guidance for where the subject may be a threat on the continuum, this is only a guide and not set in stone. The higher he or she is on the scale, the more risk they pose. Before Anderson's leave of absence, it was my expert opinion that he was approaching the "high-risk" mark, due to a clear intent to harm and his intense uncontrollable anger.

> Experts never should say definitely that a person is a threat or not a threat. Assessing their threat level using a scale is the best approach. The person's initial assessment can change depending on what happens in the person's life as he or she moves forward.[9] The low, medium, and high ranges may include the following descriptions. There are many other possibilities that may include more or even less components.

---

9 Michael Corcoran and James Cawood. *Violence Risk Assessment and Intervention: The Practitioner's Handbook*. CRC Press, 2009.

Low: The effect of violence is tightly contained with a low probability of being carried out at this time period.

Moderate: The probability of violence is increased, but the person has few resources to carry out an act of violence at this current time or a lack of certain behavior that would increase the threat level. The subject in question must be carefully watched and monitored.

High: The subject has various components in place to carry out a threat. These components can include a newly purchased gun, targeting a named person(s), and presenting an immediate threat.

We must look at the bigger picture in terms of what's going on with the individual when making an assessment. Assessment of a history of violent behavior can be somewhat subjective. Was the violence something that occurred in the recent past, or did it occur decades ago? What was the situation then compared to today? For example, was the person in a turbulent relationship? Was he or she struggling with finances or living arrangements? Has he or she attended anger management classes since then? By putting together pieces of the puzzle, you can get a better idea of whether future danger is eminent.

Due to his increase in anger, I recommended that Anderson undergo a fitness-for-duty evaluation. This fitness-for-duty *must* be done by a forensic psychologist or psychiatrist that specializes in determining potentials for violence. This is critical, as there are many licensed clinicians who perform testing, but their area of expertise has to be in predicting future violence. Anderson denied the evaluation on the basis that he would not sign a confidentiality release for the psychologist. Without this release, the psychologist was unable to perform a fitness-for-duty evaluation. I also recommended that Anderson undergo a psych exam and, pending the results, be placed under a strong supervisor with the skills to observe Anderson's behavior pattern, watching for any warning signs of potential violence. Anderson would also be required to sign a "no violence" agreement with the company. Anderson's manager needed to watch for any signs whatsoever that would require us to take more drastic steps in containing Anderson's behavior for the safety of his coworkers, himself, and anyone else.

Remember that, when assessing a threat, the period you're scrutinizing is short term. Even if an assessment reveals that the potential for violence doesn't exist today, that doesn't mean it won't exist at a later date. If you were to hire this individual, and he began acting erratically, there could be cause for concern. People's lives change: divorce, bankruptcy, infidelity, death. When changes like these occur in a person's life, it's not uncommon for someone to dive into a depressive state. And with that may come any number of behavioral or personality changes. In other words, who the person was yesterday may be completely different than who he or she is today.

Traditional Workplace Violence

Historically, security professionals and threat assessment experts concentrated on acts of violence within the workplace, which have been an issue for Americans for some years now. This kind of violence has largely been the result of something relating primarily to the worksite, occurring largely as a result of an incident with a disgruntled or psychologically disturbed worker.

In 2007, on the campus of Virginia Tech, a student named Seung-Hui Cho methodically shot and killed thirty-two people in two separate attacks two hours apart.[10] His actions were deliberate, and at one point, he even stopped to mail a package to the news media before committing suicide. As I write this, it's the second deadliest shooting incident by a single gunman in US history (surpassed only by the 2016 Orlando nightclub shooting) and one of the deadliest by a single gunman worldwide.

Cho had previously been diagnosed with a severe anxiety disorder. Because of federal privacy laws, Virginia Tech was unaware of Cho's previous diagnosis or the accommodations he had been granted at school. In 2005, Cho was accused of stalking two female students. After an investigation, a Virginia special justice declared Cho mentally ill and ordered him to attend treatment; however, because he was not institutionalized, he was still allowed to purchase guns.

In January 2017, Esteban Santiago, a former Iraq War veteran—who even after being charged with domestic battery and questioned by the FBI still had a right to carry a concealed weapon—opened fire in a Florida airport. Video footage shows him as calm and collected, even lying down on the ground for surrender—begging, it seemed, for the system to help him. Warning signs had been abundant. He had been questioned and released. He had a history of domestic violence, which has proven time and time again to be a sign that more violence is to come. We have repeatedly seen these types of warnings ignored. Studies now show that when strangulation in a domestic altercation is reported, some 90 percent of those offenders go on to kill the victim (or others) in a later altercation. Signs cannot

10 "Seung-Hui Cho Biography," accessed April 4, 2017, www.biography.com/people/seung-hui-cho-235991.

be ignored. We must train our justice system to look at these reports and place a much heavier judgment on domestic violence histories. It is becoming an all-too-familiar thread in the reports of those taking on individual terrorist acts.

In August 2010, at a distribution warehouse in Manchester, CT, another shooter, Omar Thornton, stopped between bursts of violence to make calls to his family and to state police to explain his actions. He even told the dispatcher during one of the calls that he wished he could have killed more people.

In all of these instances, the brutality was suspended long enough to make a clear-headed decision to communicate the intent with others. In Cho's case, he continued the violence after mailing the package. In a workplace shooting, the violence often begins outside the workplace—at home or on the way to the worksite—and then it ends with the shooter taking his or her own life, as happened in both the Cho and Thornton attacks.

In this regard, workplace attacks are similar to terrorism (suicide bombings), in that the attacker kills others and kills himself or herself just to make a point. The attacker/bomber is using his or her action to react against a world they feel is unjust or was unjust to them in some regard. They feel they have suffered, so they want others to suffer as well—and they want to be the one to dish out that punishment. They want to be remembered for their "payback."

That sense of justification—that they're justified in doling out retribution—is a big component of violence, from domestic violence to workplace violence to terrorism. In every situation, the blame is placed on the people attacked: "You made me do this because you treated me (or my people) unjustly."

Both workplace violence and terrorism are typically emotionless, premeditated acts—they are planned and carried out with no emotional display. The attackers typically remain calm and cool-headed, and they often act almost as if they are in another world of sorts.

New Workplace Threats

There have been few politically motivated cases of domestic terrorism, such as the Oklahoma City bombing, but in our post-9/11 world, that is changing. The December 2015 shootings in San Bernardino, CA, allegedly committed by two shooters holding allegiances to a Middle East terrorist organization, blurred the lines between terrorism and workplace violence.[11] This shooting left fourteen people dead and twenty-two seriously injured when Syed Rizwan Farook and Tashfeen Malik, a married couple living in the city of Redlands, targeted a San Bernardino County Department of Public Health training event and Christmas party of about eighty employees in a rented banquet room. After the shooting, the couple fled in a rented sport utility vehicle, only to be killed four hours later during a shootout with police.

According to former FBI Director James B. Comey, the FBI's investigation revealed that the perpetrators were "homegrown violent extremists" inspired by—but not directed by—any terrorist cell or network. FBI investigators have said Farook and Malik had become

---

11 The Federal Bureau of Investigation (FBI) defines terrorism as "the unlawful use of force or violence against persons or property to intimidate or coerce a government, the civilian population, or any segment thereof, in furtherance of political or social objectives." ("Terrorism," National Institute of Justice, modified September 13, 2011, accessed July 4, 2016, www.nij.gov/topics/crime/terrorism/pages/welcome.aspx). The Occupational Safety and Health Administration (OSHA) defines workplace violence is "any act or threat of physical violence, harassment, intimidation, or other threatening disruptive behavior that occurs at the worksite. It ranges from threats and verbal abuse to physical assaults and even homicide. It can affect and involve employees, clients, customers, and visitors." ("Safety and Health Topics," United States Department of Labor, accessed April 11, 2016, www.osha.gov/SLTC/workplaceviolence/).

radicalized over several years prior to the attack, consuming "poison on the Internet" and expressing a commitment to jihadism and martyrdom in private messages to each other.

What can security professionals and business owners learn from this scenario? That the psychological review process is as important as ever, and as the internal threats go, so must our priorities as to what we consider a terrorist expand to include new research strategies and consider the overlap of traditionally external acts that are now enacted in places of work.

Threat assessment experts must be savvier about threats from international terrorists groups alongside the more traditional workplace violence. The blurring of the lines between what has typically defined workplace violence and terrorism introduces new challenges for employers who must now walk a fine line between keeping the workplace safe while respecting the rights of current and potential employees of all nationalities. Employers cannot ignore the warning signs—domestic violence reports must be considered. While it may seem unfair to judge a person on a personal conflict, too many of those have turned into large-scale retaliations, as if the violence at home is a practice to see what they can get away with. This is not always true, of course, but it is another trigger to be aware of.

Today, employees of an organization can harbor the potential for terrorist-type violence, which may manifest itself in overt activities involving extreme religious or political beliefs. This is not about racial or religious profiling—that is, demonstrating a bias or prejudice toward people of another race/ethnicity or who have different religious beliefs. But a person in the workplace who is overly obsessed or vocal about extreme religious or political beliefs, or whose belief systems tests the limits of a supervisor's authority and control, is a matter for concern.

While terrorism in the workplace is still violence, it is treated differently by officials and by the public in general. Workplace violence has increased in the past few decades to the point that the general public is becoming somewhat desensitized to it. But since 9/11, when the label of terrorism was applied to what has typically been considered workplace violence, a new level of fear has been generated. This has caused a significant shift in the national threat assessment matrix. It's no longer enough just to address the issue of traditional workplace violence; now we as a society and those of us in the security industry especially must prepare and understand the elements of terrorism as well. We will discuss some of the indicators in the following section.

The Warning Signs

When it comes to recognizing the propensity for a violent act in your workplace, the key is to pay attention to warning signs, while also considering all pieces of the puzzle.

For instance, a history of drinking and fighting as a youth doesn't necessarily indicate a current problem. And an adult drinking on weekends doesn't mean they're going to be violent in the workplace. However, if someone with a history of violence begins to withdraw and become socially isolated or have little interaction with others, then you're looking at multiple warning signs, which may warrant a closer look, especially if that reveals the person is struggling financially or dealing with a personal issue.

This is why it's critical for you as a leader of an organization—manager, human resources professional, loss prevention, or security director—to educate yourself on human behavior. It's imperative for you to understand the trigger points that can ultimately lead to violence.

Intuition Saves Lives

So how can you take action? The first step is to teach employees how to review internal resources and encourage them to "listen to their gut." Intuition is one of the strongest tools to keep us on our toes and ready to plunge into action if necessary.

If an encounter with a coworker is escalating and your gut tells you something is not right, listen to it. If you begin to see the person pacing back and forth with a nervous edge, don't ignore it. You must address the person's growing hostility and keep your own fear and anger in check. Stay calm, empathize, and redirect to ensure they don't explode. Often, it can be helpful to utilize a personal anecdote that may or may not be even true to help them feel they have someone they can relate to, reach out to, and have access to if they feel they are hitting a limit. Even taking the time to show them something funny with an uplifting message can help change the mood of the individual without having to show that you see them in distress. This approach helps a person focus on an outside source and remember that many people feel the same way.

That brings us to the ways we can recognize bodily threats.

Physical signals are perhaps the best way to assess threats, but they're also next to impossible to identify without understanding how fear, anger, and rage affect the body.

- **Fear.** When fear kicks in, blood rushes to the large skeletal muscles (i.e., the legs, making it easier to maneuver swiftly). Either real or imagined, the fear of being attacked can escalate the rate of becoming violent.

- **Anger.** When a person reaches a point of anger, blood rushes to the hands, making it easier to engage with a weapon or fight an opponent. The heart rate increases. The rush of adrenaline triggers an action stance. Anger gives the person a feeling of energy and power. It is seductive and euphoric, which can make it very difficult to keep under control. Nevertheless, when a person experiences anger, it can be hard to control the emotions and actions. However, some kind of impulse control is usually still in place, offering an opportunity to defuse the situation.
- **Rage.** When rage is present, the person engages in negative self-talk, precipitating a higher state of anger. Once the person is in a rage, the person becomes incapable of rationalizing, and diffusing the rage becomes impossible. Asking them to sit down and talk rationally is no longer an option.

Threat assessment is a science and an art, and intuition can go a long way in helping you determine whether a situation needs further assessment.

You really must "study with vigor."[12] You must understand how the world is changing and how you can best protect your organization. In fact, when learning new ways to deal with workplace threats, you may want to employ a method known as *mind mapping*, based on Leonardo da Vinci's style of note-taking.[13] Mind mapping is a method of organizing ideas. Instead of creating a list, you typically begin by jotting down an idea on paper and then branch your thoughts out from there. You can also doodle disjointed ideas and then create branches to them later.

12 Michael Gelb, *How to Think Like Leonardo da Vinci* (New York: Dell, 2000).

13 Tony Buzan, 1960, cited in Gelb.

© Picore International

To use this method in threat assessment, you begin by placing the person of interest in the center of the page and then branch off areas of concern. For instance, you place John in the center of the page and create a branch that represents isolation. From there, you might create another branch representing an instance of isolation.

For example, Susan went up to the copy room where John works and he ignored her. That one small incident may not be a big indicator, but it may lead you to find other branches of greater significance.

This method actually works well when you have a gut feeling that something isn't right, but you can't quite put your finger on what's wrong. Everyone has bad days, but by making a diagram of your concerns, you can begin to get a picture of whether you may have a real problem on your hands. Is one employee starting to have more than a normal number of bad days? This can also help you decide whether you need to call in an expert.

Recently, my firm was called in to handle a case where an employee declared he could shoot someone. We had to investigate and assess the threat level.

The employee was isolated in the workplace. He kept to himself and didn't really interact. Then one day someone asked him how he was doing and he blurted out, "I'm just so frustrated I could shoot somebody. I'm really serious about this." The other employee took his concerns to the supervisor, leaving the supervisor with a quandary. What was he to do?

Often, the first recourse when someone blurts out a threat is to suspend the person pending an investigation, but that can also create immediate havoc. In this instance, the supervisor called in an expert rather than dealing with the employee directly.

We advised the company to leave the employee on the floor, and we sent in a plain-clothes executive protection agent to blend in. Armed with a concealed weapon, the agent was instructed to act casually after arriving at the facility. The manager was asked to bring the employee into his office, where he was handed a phone to talk to me. I then asked him specific questions to help determine whether he presented a real threat. The results of that phone call determined subsequent steps.

This case was initially moderate on the threat assessment scale. If there had been knowledge of easy access to a weapon, then the threat would have been high. However, after talking to the individual, the threat level was decreased from moderate to low. One benefit to years of industry work is being able to assess a situation and know how to gauge the potential for a rise in threat versus a downgrade. This takes years of practice; however, with proper training, you too can learn to recognize a possible threat and determine whether you can handle it on your own or need the assistance of a professional.

If something like this happens at your company, you should wait for covert security to arrive before approaching the employee. Why? Because it's possible that the employee already has a weapon on-site and is prepared to use it. In some open-carry states, it's actually legal for the employee to already have a weapon at his disposal.

You also should not call the employee into your office and start your own internal investigation. Call an expert, and let the expert create the strategy on how to defuse the situation, even if that means calling law enforcement.

Scott Hewitt, former director of security for a major company, worked closely with my firm on many cases where we would brainstorm on, first, what the threat level was, then how to best defuse the threat level and contain any possible violence. It is critical that one not think about how something would impact themselves as they are thinking rationally. We must think how something will affect the subject of interest, who is not always thinking rationally. It was Scott's open mindedness that allowed mind mapping to work in order to think of alternative solutions to create boundaries for the subject and keep him/her from acting out.

Can't Happen Here

As a leader, you can no longer afford to ignore changes in the workplace. Too often, we hear after the fact that the attacker "was a great guy" or "wasn't the type who would do something like this." Too often, people downplay uncertain behaviors; they think that the person next to them is different, but he would never turn violent—"he's just not the type." Don't believe that what you read on the news couldn't happen at your company.

While it's true that the majority of workplaces will never experience news-headlining acts of violence, the potential for violence is no longer something that can be ignored. You must be attuned to what's going on in your workplace; you don't need to be paranoid, but you must be prepared to proactively approach issues of concern. This begins by educating yourself on potential indicators of workplace violence and terrorism.

The personality theorist Walter Mischel suggested that behavior is dependent on situational cues rather than on certain traits.[14] In other words, with so many variables involved, it's hard to assume that a person is going to react the same way every time they encounter a situation. Mischel's theory found "if-then" patterns between situations and behaviors; for instance, if situation *x* occurs, then behavior *y* may be the result. For instance, a person may engage in drug use when in the company of other drug users, but may stop using in a different environment. In other words, even if he or she has an addictive personality trait, his or her drug use may rely entirely on the company or the environment in which he or she lives.

---

14 "Mischel's Cognitive-Affective Model of Personality and the Person-Situation Debate," accessed April 4, 2017, www.boundless.com/psychology/textbooks/boundless-psychology-textbook/personality-16/social-cognitive-perspectives-on-personality-81/mischel-s-cognitive-affective-model-of-personality-and-the-person-situation-debate-315-12850/

Based on this theory, it's conceivable that removing a person from a situation where they exhibit potentially violent behaviors to an environment that is less stressful or threatening to them may decrease the potential for violence. For instance, if a person with poor impulse control is working in an environment where he or she is being taunted or mistreated, the potential for violence may be greater than if that person were in a more supportive work environment where people expressed appreciation for that person's contributions. This is why it is important for managers in organizations to respect people they oversee and for coworkers to respect each other. For some people, especially those who lack impulse control and who have serious mental or substance abuse issues, bad behavior on the part of a coworker or supervisor may be all it takes to push them to that place where violence is their recourse. In other words, keeping someone in a negative environment, one that is causing the behavioral problem, makes it more likely that the person will explode one day.

What Can Be Done!

One of the best ways to deter violence in the workplace is through preemployment background checks.

> **Note**: Juvenile criminal records are closed, and employers cannot use anything that happened more than seven years prior as a reason for non-hire. However, having information about a person from prior years can empower you with information about that person's personality and prompt you to be more watchful.
>
> It's critical to run a social trace and process backgrounds in every state/county that the person lived in. The social trace will show many of the places where the employee candidate lived. A general

background won't capture all of the possible criminal cases, if any, that the subject may have.

For former military personnel, request a DD Form 214, a veteran's military discharge, or separation documents. This can help you see whether a veteran's discharge was honorable or dishonorable. It can also give you insight into his or her military record—was he or she a cook or an explosives expert? Did he or she receive any medals or specialized training?

During the interview, be sure to ask candidates questions to give you insight into how they handle conflict in their former workplace. Ask them questions you're legally allowed to ask: for example, how they handled or defused a previous conflict with a coworker or a supervisor. In addition to listening to what they have to say, watch their facial expressions and body language.

The Interview

Some critical questions to ask are:

- Tell me about yourself.
- What are character traits that your former coworkers would use to describe you?
- Who are your heroes?
- What is the one thing you would like to achieve if you get this job?
- What attracted you to this company?
- What are the three things you disliked about your last job?
- What are the skills necessary for this job?

- Why are you leaving your last job?
- Why are you leaving your former employer?
- How would you describe your work style?
- Can you describe a time when your work was criticized?
- How do you work with people who annoy you?
- If I was your supervisor and asked you to do something that you disagreed with, what would you do?
- Why should I hire you?
- How do you want to improve yourself in the next year?

Briana Morgaine described seventy-three questions that would be good to ask employees during an interview. I selected a few of these questions that you can concentrate on as you delve deeper into the potential employee's psyche when deciding to hire or not to hire. Selecting the right person for the job pertaining to his/her skill level is, of course, important, but equally important is how this employee fits into the corporate culture: what is his/her temperament, what can we learn about this person, and how does he/she handle stress? All of these questions can help you understand the applicant and if there may be potential issues of concern down the line.

CHAPTER 3

Major Mental Illness and Personality Disorders

Several years ago, my firm got a worried call from a television personality (I'll call him Dan), who suspected he was being stalked. The stalker was a twenty-year-old (I'll call her Beth) who lived six hours from Dan but would fly to his home and leave gifts on the doorstep.

It was a long and relatively expensive trip for Beth to make, and this coupled with her ability to take time off work from a full-time job to make the trip and her ability to find out where Dan lived showed that she was smart, resourceful, and had some means.

Beth hadn't shown any violent or menacing tendencies, but her actions were still disturbing. When a person travels a great distance from one city to another and drop off flowers at a person's home that they don't know, it is disturbing. When the one being stalked first realizes that the stalker thinks they are in a relationship with a TV personality, it gets dangerous. We frequently hear of people stalking celebrities. Perhaps most famously was the murder of the pop singer Selena by a fan and business associate, whom no one suspected of any such tendencies. You may also recall the incident with astronaut Lisa

Nowak, who drove nonstop wearing a diaper to allegedly kidnap and murder the girlfriend of her former coworker and love interest. This was another situation of a person no one thought would have the capacity for such an attempted atrocity, and it is why threat assessors take stalking situations very seriously.

As such, we had a surveillance team follow Beth to monitor her behavior and assess the threat level and to get an up close and personal assessment. I went undercover, posing as one of Dan's assistants and invited Beth to a meeting. The "assistant" called from a blocked number so Beth would not know who the caller was. Prior to the call, we developed a script to stay on point. During the call, I made small talk. At first, Beth said she was trying to reach the TV personality and that in order to talk to him, she must first meet with his personal assistant. Initially, Beth appeared to be an average person. She talked about where she worked and a little bit about her life, explaining that she worked for a major university as an office assistant. But it quickly became clear that the threat level was not low, by any means. She clearly suffered from some sort of delusion, though we didn't diagnose her mental disorder (best left to clinical professionals who can diagnose and treat her while being assessed in person with clinical tests to assist with the DX). I did, however, challenge her fantasy relationship and told her not to contact Dan again. She became flustered, her thoughts became disjointed, she couldn't keep track of her story, and she started to display obvious signs of agitation and anxiety. By the end of the meeting, she was in a seriously disoriented state. The team escorted her to the airport, but along the way she weaved in and out of cars, stopping and starting erratically. She boarded a flight home and never returned to Dan's home.

Mental disorders are something we look for in potentially dangerous people. Though it's the subject of ongoing debate, a mental disorder does not necessarily mean someone's going to be violent. However, there is always a threat to consider when one's mental stability can be triggered by a stimulus that most would not react to at all, or at least not as severely.

Stalking victims had little protection until the anti-stalking laws were enacted in the early 1990s and then improved in the following years.[15] By 1994, laws in California stated that any person who willfully, maliciously, and repeatedly follows or harasses another person and who makes a credible threat with the intent to place that person in reasonable fear for his or her safety, or the safety of his or her immediate family, for fifteen minutes or more is guilty of the crime of stalking.

Tatiana Tarasoff is a prime example of a stalking victim who would have benefited from the law. She was a student attending the University of California Berkeley. All she did was share a friendly kiss with the subject, Prosenjit Poddar, after a short time dating. Poddar interpreted their relationship as serious—a feeling not shared by Tarasoff. She told him that she was dating other men and was not interested in a serious relationship. He thought they were in love and could not accept the rejection. He became obsessed with Tarasoff and openly expressed to his psychologist his intentions to kill her. The psychologist believed he was suffering from paranoid schizophrenia and informed the campus police of Poddar's voiced threat. The school police interviewed Poddar and determined that he was not dangerous. However, Poddar issued more threats against her until

---

15 Robert N. Miller, "'Stalk Talk': A First Look at Anti-Stalking Legislation," *Washington and Lee Law Review* vol. 50, no. 3, http://scholarlycommons.law.wlu.edu/cgi/viewcontent.cgi?article=1775&context=wlulr.

he went to Tarasoff's house and shot her with a pellet gun, before stabbing her fourteen times with a kitchen knife he was carrying. He turned himself in and was convicted of murder (though later released on a technicality and sent to live in India). As a result of this case, psychotherapists must now report any threats to police and to the victim as well.

Although mental illness is not the primary indicator that an individual will resort to violence, a 1990 epidemiological study by psychiatry and behavioral sciences professor Jeff Swanson at Duke University revealed that individuals with a diagnosis of a major mental disorder do report more violence (i.e., bipolar disorder, major depression, compulsive disorder, schizophrenia, etc.).

However, the MacArthur Violence Risk Assessment[16] found a number of flaws with extant research. The MacArthur study found that 31 percent of people with a dual-diagnosis—for instance, a psychiatric disorder along with substance abuse—committed at least one act of violence in a year, compared to 18 percent of people with a psychiatric disorder alone. The study confirms that while some people with mental disorders do commit violence, mental disorder alone doesn't mean that a person will be violent. Rather, aggression stems from multiple overlapping factors interacting in complex ways.

> "People discharged from psychiatric hospitals" is not a homogeneous category regarding violence. People with a major mental disorder diagnosis and without a substance abuse diagnosis are involved in significantly less community violence than are people with a co-occurring substance abuse diagnosis.

---

16 "Violence: The MacArthur Community Violence Study," MacArthur Research Network on Mental Health and the Law, accessed April 4, 2017, www.macarthur.virginia.edu/mentalhome.html.

> The prevalence of violence among people who have been discharged from a hospital and who do not have symptoms of substance abuse is about the same as the prevalence of violence among other people living in their communities who do not have symptoms of substance abuse.
>
> The prevalence of violence is higher among people—discharged psychiatric patients or non-patients—who have symptoms of substance abuse. People who have been discharged from a psychiatric hospital are more likely than other people living in their communities to have symptoms of substance abuse.
>
> The prevalence of violence among people who have been discharged from a psychiatric hospital and who have symptoms of substance abuse is significantly higher than the prevalence of violence among other people living in their communities who have symptoms of substance abuse, for the first several months after discharge.
>
> Violence committed by people discharged from a hospital is very similar to violence committed by other people living in their communities in terms of type (i.e., hitting), target (i.e., family members), and location (i.e., at home).[17]

Scientific studies can offer insight into violent behavior, but the controversial nature of the field is another reason why knowledge must be combined with experience when identifying potential treats and knowing when to bring in an expert. Here again is further proof that there's an art to threat assessment.

---

17 H. Steadman, E. Mulvey, J. Monahan, P. Robbins, P. Appelbaum, T. Grisso, L. Roth, & E. Silver. "Violence by People Discharged from Acute Psychiatric Inpatient Facilities and by Others in the Same Neighborhoods," *Archives of General Psychiatry* 55, (1998): 393–401.

Murderous Intent and Overlapping Factors

Robert Bardo. After stalking the actress Rebecca Schaeffer in July 1989, Robert Bardo shot and killed Schaeffer when she answered the door to her Los Angeles apartment.

Mark Chapman. In December 1980, Mark Chapman shot and killed John Lennon outside the musician's New York City apartment.

John Hinckley. In March 1981, John Hinckley attempted to assassinate US President Ronald Reagan outside a hotel in Washington, DC.

These three murderers had traits in common leading up to their murderous acts. All three were obsessed with the J.D. Salinger's *Catcher in the Rye*, a fictional book about a troubled adolescent. Now, if an individual in a corporation had a copy of that book on their desk, would that mean he or she is a potential threat? Not necessarily. But if that same individual gained the attention of a company leader because of some other questionable or negative act—maybe angry outbursts or threatening language—and it was known or discovered that he/she had a dog-eared copy of the book on hand, then the situation is one that potentially warrants a closer look.

This is why security professionals look for common traits in people who are potentially dangerous. Not only does looking at the suspect in question provide valuable knowledge when assessing a potential threat, but this knowledge may also trigger recall of commonalities with already convicted murders. Noticing these commonalities will help a security professional make a better assessment.

Traits common among people ultimately convicted of murder or attempts to kill include:

- **Stressful early life experiences.** Many people who commit violence later in life experienced adversity as a child. Often, the adversity comes from a dysfunctional home life or even physical harm at the hands of an adult.
- **Predatory behavior.** Stalking a target is common among people who ultimately murder.
- **Keeping a diary or writing letters.** Many people keep diaries and write letters, but assassin personalities often write out the fantasies they want to act out.
- **Selling off personal possessions.** People planning for a big event—such as potentially suicide or incarceration—may sell off or give away all their personal belongings and even close their bank accounts.
- **Purchasing a weapon.** Many people purchase weapons for any number of reasons. For would-be assassins, this act is part of a to-do list.
- **Obsession with murder.** Killers are often found to be obsessed with the prior acts of serial killers or others convicted of heinous or news-making murders.
- **Obsession with celebrities.** With Bardo, Chapman, and Hinckley, celebrities held their attention. They were obsessed with their victims and researched them thoroughly, tracking their victims as they moved in the public eye.

Make no mistake, people with mental disorders—and murderous intent—are typically smart and often highly creative people. They often have to be in order to circumvent security measures.

Their obsession with murder often includes identifying with either another stalker or murder to the point of actually copying the behavior of their idol.

I would like to add a brief description of the successful terrorist as well as our traditional workplace violence subject and our well-known stalkers.

A terrorist must be dedicated. To be successful he cannot be a part-time mercenary; he/she must become a *fedayeen*, a man or woman of sacrifice, with obedience to the leader.

Personal bravery. The terrorist must face the possibility of death, injury, imprisonment, or even torture if captured. He must not have our basic human emotions of pity or remorse since most situations will involve innocent adults and children.

Fairly high standard of intelligence. High degree of sophistication in order to blend into society and well educated and possessing a fair share of general knowledge. This criteria was presented by Edgar O'Ballance in the book *The Language of Violence: The Blood Politics of Terrorism.*

There is much debate over what is considered workplace violence or terrorism. Classic workplace violence and terrorism are becoming increasingly similar. Terrorism is becoming more like those seen in incidents of workplace and or school violence and less like those associated with highly coordinated acts of terrorism. The lone wolf terrorists pose a security threat equal to that of Al-Qaeda. Many were born and raised in the United States and come from middle-class backgrounds. The most important point to remember is that it's not your job to decide what you are dealing with. Just know that the behavior is troubling and report it to your supervisor immediately and bring in a threat assessment consultant to assess the situation properly.

To Intervene or Not to Intervene . . .

In Dan's case, after examining the evidence and consulting an interdisciplinary team of experts, we made the decision to contact Beth in order to assess the threat. But interventions don't always work; they can backfire and escalate to violence. A restraining order is a form of intervention, but this, too, can backfire.

There is no easy way to determine whether implementing surveillance is a best course of action—it's only one of many possible types of interventions that could be effective in the right situation. In a workplace setting, it's best to employ an interdisciplinary team to deal with a suspicious individual. The interdisciplinary team typically should involve legal and human resources and threat assessment professionals. Meeting with the individual is nearly always best done off-site. If the suspicious employee is suspended pending an investigation, he or she should not be brought back to the workplace for any reason until the risk he or she poses is determined to be low.

The Psychopath

One personality that is difficult to spot, but which is one of the most dangerous to deal with, is the psychopath. And psychopaths are far more violent than nonpsychopathic criminals. In diagnosing a psychopath, mental health professionals use the Hare Psychopathy Checklist-Revised (PCL-R) developed by Robert Hare, Ph.D. The checklist was originally created to assess criminal behaviors, but today it is often used by qualified examiners to determine the presence and level of psychopathy in a person.[18] You may be able to identify someone you suspect to be a psychopath if he or she:

---

18 "Hare Psychopathy Checklist," *Encyclopedia of Mental Disorders*, accessed July 4, 2016, www.minddisorders.com/Flu-Inv/Hare-Psychopathy-Checklist.html

- is glib or superficially charming
- has a grandiose sense of self-worth
- is found to lie pathologically
- is a con artist or is manipulative
- lacks remorse or guilt
- is shallow
- lacks empathy
- is impulsive

Paranoid Delusions

Paranoia is another mental condition that can make a person a threat. Paranoid people often appear angry at the world. They distrust people and feel that they are susceptible to deception. This type of individual will predominantly be on the defensive and ready for an encounter with the perceived enemy.

As with any psychiatric disorder, when assessing a threatening situation in which the person appears paranoid or delusional, resist the temptation to use clinical terminology, in this case, "paranoid." Only a licensed mental health care provider is capable of making an accurate diagnosis, so it is best to frame the situation by the person's actions; is he or she acting suspicious, distrusting, or fearful? Nevertheless, paranoia often causes delusions or hallucinations, some of which can be cause for concern. Does the person claim the Martians are coming? Are they being told by voices to hurt someone? The latter, called command hallucinations, tell someone to undertake a harmful action and are very concerning. Like Esteban Santiago of the Ft. Lauderdale airport shooting who reported hearing violent commands, the person can't fight against the voices.

When we assess someone who says they're hearing voices, we ask, "What are the voices saying?" If beings are coming for a visit from outer space, that's one thing. But if the voices are saying, "Kill John the manager tomorrow because he's a bad person," then we have a situation on our hands that requires immediate action.

My firm had one case where the employee didn't see images or hear voices, but she saw everyday annoyances as a direct threat to her, such as someone taking too long at the gas station or cutting her off in traffic. We all experience these types of annoyances but this employee believed "they" were out to upset her life. She was assessed as a low-to-moderate threat because she did not intend harm to anyone in her immediate surroundings but did want "them" to stop harassing her. I also made sure there were no voices telling her to harm anyone, which would have increased the risk to "high."

According to a newly released police affidavit, just ten days before Christmas 2016, a Texas man named Craig Vandewege fatally slashed the throats of his wife and infant son. Days before, he had allegedly told coworkers that he heard voices telling him to "kill people" and had dreamed of hurting his spouse. At one point, he told someone that he planned on meeting with then-President-elect Donald Trump to talk about the killings. His wife Shanna and their son, Deidrick, were found in the master bedroom of their home with apparent knife wounds to their necks. What might have been the outcome had Vandewege's company done more to train their employees in threat assessment and communication? We'll never know for sure, but I suspect it might have helped in saving Shanna and Deidrick's lives.

Measuring Risk

Actuarial tests, which are used by mental health professionals, can help assess risk. As risk assessment instruments, they may add additional insight to clinical judgment as long as the tools are used in the hands of someone who was trained and skilled with such tools. For instance, the Spousal Assault Risk Assessment Guide (SARA) is a checklist for case managers to use in determining the risk for violence that may occur as a result of assault by a spouse. The Historical Clinical Risk Management-20 (HCR-20) is another evaluation tool used by mental health professionals to determine the best treatment and management strategies for mentally ill individuals who have the potential to become violent. Results from the evaluation can be used to predict a person's future inclination toward violence. However, the HCR-20 is not intended to be a standalone tool, and it should only be administered by professionals trained in conducting individual assessments to determine threat types.

For non-experts in this specialized area of concern, learning how threat assessment experts and security professionals as well as mental health professionals manage threats and rate threats from low, moderate, or high can assist you in deciding when to bring in an expert or assess if you currently have enough knowledge to manage the case on your own. Mind you that a threat level can change from one level to another depending on what is happening to the person in his/her life at any one time. Whether as an individual or a business owner, you can utilize your own internal threat level system once you understand these different types of threat levels.

Threat Types

All threats are not created equal. Some may be direct, while others may be indirect. But more than likely, a threatening statement or action will raise our awareness enough to know that a situation may be dangerous. Those who make these types of threats are typically triggered by a stressor that escalates into additional stress, anxiety, and/or depression for them.

Indirect threats can range from low to high. Indirect threats are vague or veiled; someone may issue a threat without actually being specific, but the intent of the threat is understood. For instance, someone may utter statements such as: "I could kill you if I wanted to," "Oh, you haven't seen me angry yet," "Do you know why I spent time in an institution (or jail)?" "Here's the phone; come on, call for help." There are many variables that need to be assessed before we rate a threat.

Direct threats can range from low to high and involve a specific, identifiable risk. With direct threats, assessment looks at the duration of the risk, the nature and severity of potential harm, the likelihood that the potential harm is immediate, and whether the risk is current, remote, speculative, or future based. For instance, someone may say: "I will kill you," "If I go down, you go down," or, "This is what you get for firing me." In the case of the latter, those were the last words uttered by Paul Calden, claims manager for Fireman's Fund Insurance, who, in 1993, returned to the cafeteria of his former employer and began shooting. Three people died in that incident, and Calden fled in a car, only to commit suicide in a park.

In addition to the type of communication, you could be dealing with one of three different types of threats with different traits, ranking from low to high.

- **Low:** Indirect or veiled threats are considered low risk. Low-risk threat tendencies lean toward agitation, one or two angry outbursts, blaming others, excessive use of profanity, a sense of entitlement, being argumentative, inappropriate use of company equipment, or long-term ownership of a firearm at home. Someone who exhibits these behaviors is a concern, but is not automatically classified as dangerous.
- **Moderate:** Moderate threats are increasing in specificity. A moderate risk level may be a combination of an indirect threat, such as uttering a threatening statement, combined with a second behavior such as slamming doors or throwing items. Other traits include repeated angry outbursts, a repeated pattern of harassment, unacceptable physical actions short of body contact (for example, blocking someone's path to an exit or throwing an item such as a pen across the room). Moderate may also include body contact such as bumping into a person or putting a hand on someone's shoulder to confront them, saying something like, "Hey buddy, I was talking to you."
- **High:** High-level risk includes conditional threats or ultimatums, such as uttering a phrase like, "If you don't give me that raise, I will kill you." High-risk threats suggest someone is growing more physically violent, usually following clear and direct threats. High-risk threats may include a receipt in someone's desk indicating they just bought a handgun. This is different from someone who hunts and whom you know owns or collects guns. Intense preoccupation with weapons to a level that would

make another gun owner uneasy is a high-risk indicator. A sudden, escalating interest in guns along with increased visits to a gun range indicates heightening risk.

So now that you know the different threat types, you need to take that knowledge and begin a strategy for scenarios that you may encounter. We call this the "what if" when doing training. It is a useful tool when training that can be attributed to multiple facets one faces in work and in life.

What Can Be Done!

If you're experiencing someone in the workplace who you feel is suffering from some type of delusion or disorientation, call the local police department and ask them to send someone to assess the individual. If you suspect an employee of a mental imbalance, don't fire them; suspend them pending an investigation.

In California, the police can determine whether they will book the person under article 5150 of the Welfare and Institutions Code (WIC). That code indicates that the police feel the person is a danger to others or to himself or herself. Under this code, the police can take the person to an institution where they will be held for up to seventy-two hours to be assessed by a psychiatric team about their level of danger to self or others. Each state has its own laws about psychiatric holds, a.k.a. involuntary civil commitment.

Whatever you do as the manager in an organization, don't just send someone home in an obviously distressed condition. Call the police and let them come in and assess the situation. When the police arrive at the workplace, if the individual causing the problem is lucid enough to explain that they're just having a stressful day, the police may let that person stay at the worksite.

You can also improve your ability to deal with a threatening situation if you "harden the target." That can be done by adding certain security measures to your operations to better protect against violent acts. Here are a few key measures you can install if you need to harden the target.

- closed-circuit television monitoring system
- "No trespass" signs
- swipe card system
- better lighting and spotlights on driveways and key doorways
- alarm system (or upgrade the existing one)
- active control lighting
- window film to keep people from seeing inside your organization
- access control doors to keep people from entering past a receptionist
- face-recognition cameras
- panic alarms at access points, especially in the reception area and parking areas
- sound and light diversions, which can disrupt an attacker's ability to think straight
- strategic use of shrubbery
- transparent weather vestibules at building entrances
- hostile vehicle mitigation (HVM). This is a general term that covers a suite of protective measures that are often employed around buildings. This can stop a vehicular

explosive device. The HVM device can also be used to protect against ram raids against high-net-worth clients such as jewelers, cash and valuables in transit depots, etc.

Example: The 2016 Nice attack when a nineteen-ton cargo truck was deliberately driven into crowds of people celebrating Bastille Day on the Promenade des Anglais in Nice. The driver was Mohamed Lahouaiej-Bouhlel.

CHAPTER 4

Relationship and Employment Instability

As we discussed in chapter 1, law enforcement officers are far from immune to stress and violence at home and in the workplace. The stress and traumatic scenes that they encounter every day can certainly take a toll on themselves as much as the people around them.

In one particular domestic violence case I worked years ago, the victim was actually a police officer, whom I'll call Jane, and was allegedly being abused by her domestic partner, Linda. The two argued a lot and Jane's unemployed partner continued to verbally abuse her between arguments. When she was in uniform and on patrol, Jane was in full control, but in her own home life, she was far from in charge.

Domestic violence occurs when the abuser believes that the abuse is acceptable, justified, or unlikely to be reported. The victims are trapped through power and control. Linda would strike out and say something abusive and then hit Jane.

Linda could get furious about anything and start to yell and kick things. She called Jane names because she couldn't find the right sauce for the pasta.

The very first action I suggested to Jane was to remove all of her weapons from the house. While talking to Jane, I tried to reframe the situation and guide her to how successful she would be when she left the relationship, and even though she might feel powerless or fearful (which was normal), she could not let it control her.

Many victims of domestic violence live in a type of isolation. They live a life that on the outside doesn't reflect the realities of life at home. They often feel a disconnect even with themselves, feeling empowered or strong at work and then demeaned and restricted in their home life. Recently, there was a campaign called "Why I Stayed" and it was an eye-opening discussion, the first of its kind for many.

Similarly themed campaigns continue to stay in the media with growing backlash for the lack of accountability for those accused. For example, a very well-known and respected Hollywood actor accused of domestic violence had his Disney movie contract extended and won a 2016 People's Choice Award. The 2017 Academy Awards season was rife with controversy when the Best Actor award was given to someone who was formally accused of sexual harassment by two different women, settled the suits, and yet still won the award. Not to mention the nomination of a best director who had committed a public display of violence and had a reported history of domestic violence. The public support around those accused can leave victims afraid to speak out because of the fear of being labeled as liars or worse—fear of verbal or physical retaliation.

People stay in difficult relationships for many reasons. They blame themselves, they hope the person will change, they don't have the means to leave, they fear for their lives or the lives of their children. To say that people "want" to be in a situation that inflicts pain and fear—be it emotional or physical—is to completely undermine what domestic violence really is. Too often, the court system fails to support the victim. Even with restraining orders in place, a piece of paper is easily ignored by someone who is used to being in charge and having control over another person's life.

While each scenario is different, there are steps to be taken that transcend them all. In this particular situation, we found Jane a shelter where she could be safe and get counseling while the restraining order was served upon Linda. There is always a risk that the violence will get worse once a restraining order is served upon the batterer, but that does not mean that you don't get one. It means you prepare for the worse while you are getting out of the relationship.

To help cope with the situation, we spoke with Jane's commanding officer to secure a week's paid leave so she could gather her thoughts together and move somewhere safe. She was moved to another station so Linda would not know her schedule, where she worked, or where she lived.

For better and for worse, domestic relationships sometimes spill over into the workplace. Strong social networks at home and at work can deter individuals from violent behavior. However, perceiving the difference between appearance and the reality at home can be deceiving. While a person may seem to have a stable home life and healthy friendships and outside interests, some actually live a life of isolation. Some people with personality disorders can find it difficult to maintain high-functioning relationships, and the resulting isolation can cause chemical changes in the brain that can affect his or her ability to regulate emotions—including those that lead to violence.

As a business owner, you might find that these tendencies exist in an employee with a history of job-hopping, as it often indicates lack of emotional control or violent tendencies that mean he or she can only hold down multiple, short-term positions. Employment instability is not necessarily an indicator of violence, and more and more milennials change jobs frequently, but job-hopping can at least give you an indication of a person's personality. It's nearly impossible to discern why an employee has a history of jumping from one employer to another; in fact, for legal reasons, past employers do not give details of why an employee no longer works for them. Typically, they're only able to confirm employment dates, positions the person held, and sometimes whether or not the person is eligible for rehire.

Nevertheless, if you find one of your employees has become threatening at home or at work, you can protect yourself by obtaining restraining orders, stay-away letters, or police reports.

If you suspect someone in your workplace is in an abusive relationship, here are a few statements you can use to offer support:

- "It's not your fault he treats you that way."
- "I know this is difficult to discuss, but please know you can talk to me about anything."
- "You are not alone. I care about you and am here for you, no matter what."
- "You are not responsible for his behavior."
- "No matter what you did, you do not deserve this."
- "I'm here to help and am always available, even if you don't want to talk about it."
- "Remember, you're not alone. I am here for you when you're ready to talk about it."

As an employer, you need to get HR involved and be careful not to cross the boundaries; but remember, you must do something because domestic violence spill-over is a real threat in any workplace. Don't try to make any decisions for the person, because it implies that you think he or she is incapable of making good choices and it may deter him or her from confiding in you in the future. Instead, focus on offering support and encouragement. By no means am I saying that a police report should not be filed. What I am saying is proper precautions must be in place before the police make contact with the subject. In an immediate life-threatening situation, contact should be made immediately by calling 911 and/or a panic button.

Restraining Orders

Often, younger officers will automatically counsel an individual or corporation to "just get a restraining order." They'll do this for workplace restraining orders and individual restraining orders, without really explaining the pros and the cons of implementing such a tool. However, a more seasoned officer will know that in some situations restraining orders can backfire.

Restraining orders are usually issued against the batterer, who generally doesn't want to be controlled—they want to be in control of the victim. In domestic violence situations in particular, the batterer feels the restraining order is a tool to control them, so a legal document telling him or her otherwise may be perceived as a threat. In fact, a 1998 nationwide study on stalking found that 69 percent of women and 81 percent of men who took out a restraining order reported that the order was violated.[19] One problem is that restraining orders must list all the addresses from which the restrained party must stay away—and sharing this information can leave the victim of a threat even more vulnerable.

19 Patricia Tjaden and Nancy Thoennes, "Stalking in America: Findings From the National Violence Against Women Survey," *US Department of Justice*, April 1998, www.ncjrs.gov/pdffiles/169592.pdf.

I have found restraining orders to be most helpful with individuals who have a higher level of functionality. People who have acted aggressively but not violently are less likely to become violent if a restraining order is issued against them; they tend to abide by the restraining order more than someone who doesn't function well among others. A restraining order may keep a rational, previously nonviolent person at bay, but a nonviolent person may not need a restraining order in the first place.

Deciding on a restraining order requires careful thought. It's important for the restrainer to fully understand the pros and cons of the decision and not think that the document gives them a security blanket—that piece of paper doesn't guarantee that a stalker will be kept at bay.

The same holds true for restraining orders issued by corporations. A corporation can take out a general restraining order to try on some level to protect the workplace. Sometimes, one can be required for legal reasons. As a company leader, however, a restraining order on its own is no guarantee of stopping workplace violence, but there are times when it can be beneficial. Each state has its own laws regarding how this can be enforced, and as such we would recommend that you read up on this per your own states laws.

Stay-Away Letter

An alternative to a restraining order is the stay-away letter. This less-invasive option may be used when a former employee returns to the workplace after being given instructions to stay away. The letter may encourage the former employee to respect the organization's request going forward. To have the greatest impact, the letter should maintain a tone of respect and recognize the former employee may need to talk, while creating boundaries. For instance, the letter could read: "I encourage you to share with me your concerns over the matter of your dismissal. Please call so we can discuss the matter privately."

Police Report

Since a police report is usually required when an employee incident occurs, there are a few things to consider before calling the police. First, consider the timing. Similar to a restraining order, a police report could escalate the individual's propensity for violence, empowering him or her to do more harm. Knowing where you will be when the report is filed and where you can go after the fact is essential—especially if children are involved. Carefully assess each instance and each individual separately before taking the action of filing a police report. You might just want to call the police and make a general report without filing an official report, but ask for extra patrol of the area. This decision should only be made with a threat assessment expert consulting on the case.

What Factors to Assess

When assessing a potentially threatening individual, look at the support group around him or her. While isolation increases the probability of violence, studies have shown that interacting with a social support group can guard against a tendency for a person to be violent. However, what are those relationships like? Does the person have family? Does he or she live alone? Is this person an adult—in their twenties, thirties, or forties—who still lives with Mom and Dad? In my experience, I have found a number of cases where there was a higher tendency for the person to commit violence if he or she still lived at home. The person lacked connections with others outside the family, and he or she lacked the social skills to interact with the world. As society changes, more and more people are living at home for longer periods of time. This adds seclusion when their only outlet becomes social media, a source for even more anger and rage.

If the individual in question has a spouse and/or children, what are those relationships like? Is there any domestic violence occurring in the household? Does the individual have friends at or outside of work? Does he or she have a supportive family? All of this information is important when assessing the potential for an individual to be violent.

Men who are abusive within their relationships have an elevated risk of being violent outside of relationships as well. When evaluating an individual known for domestic violence, there are a few points to consider. Does the batterer resolve conflict with intimidation or bullying? Is the person verbally abusive? Domestic violence often starts with some level of verbal intimidation: "How come my soup isn't hotter? You know I like my steak rare; how come it's medium-rare?" The abuser finds reasons to be abusive and uses threats and intimidation as instruments of controlling the person. He or she may also use symbolic violence—tearing up a wedding photo, for example. Jealously is another tool of the abuser; he or she may exercise jealousy to keep their mate on a tightrope. That may include keeping the female partner from being close to her family or siblings. Sometimes, the batterer's tendencies are fueled by alcohol or drugs.

Interestingly, unemployed men tend to be less violent in relationships. When the woman has a job and the man doesn't, he tends to be less violent because he needs her.

Between 2004 and 2011, researchers from the Universities of London and Munich conducted a study of twenty thousand people in England and Wales.[20] Five percent of the people studied had experienced abuse, and around one-third of those were men who had experienced verbal abuse. The study found that a 3.7 percent increase in unemployment among men correlated with a 12 percent decrease in domestic violence. The study also found that an increase of 3 percent unemployment among women correlated to a 10 percent increase in domestic violence. The study did not directly correlate the reports of domestic violence to a person's frustration over their partner's unemployment, but it did find the following:

> When male unemployment in an area is high, more men—having either lost their jobs or fearing job loss—are likely to try to stick with their partners in order to ensure some semblance of income stability. And to keep their partners from leaving them, those that have abusive tendencies are more likely to abstain from violent behavior. Meanwhile, when female unemployment is high, women might similarly be less likely to leave men who are predisposed to abuse, and so reports of domestic violence would rise.

All acts of domestic violence are high-level threats on the threat assessment scale because of the intimate, emotional connection involved. The connection is different from the relationship between a supervisor and employee in the workplace. There is a lot more at stake in an intimate partner violence situation.

As a company leader, you can recognize signs of abuse: a woman may wear long sleeves or a turtleneck on a very hot summer day to cover bruises or other signs of abuse, or she might exhibit increased

20 Olga Khazan, "When Male Unemployment Rises, Domestic Violence Rates Fall," *The Atlantic*, August 6, 2013, www.theatlantic.com/international/archive/2013/08/when-male-unemployment-rises-domestic-violence-rates-fall/278423/

absenteeism, low self-esteem, a need for approval, or physical symptoms, such as repeated headaches, anxiety, and stomach pains.

Signs Someone Is Being Battered

- appears to be trusting, has low self-esteem, and shows a significant need for recognition, approval, and affection
- is nonaggressive, dependent, powerless, and isolated
- shows physical symptoms, including headaches, anxiety, stomach pains, and bruises
- has mysterious cuts or bruises and heavy makeup
- wears long sleeves on hot days

Don't be fooled into thinking that someone couldn't be an abuser—domestic violence happens in all economic segments, from the maintenance worker to an executive in your organization. Even police officers have been involved in workplace violence with their spouses. They will go to work and put a gun on and protect the world, but when they go home they themselves become the person others need to be protected from. High-profile celebrities can also attest to this. A few weeks after the 2009 Grammys, photos were released of R&B singer Rihanna after she had been assaulted by her boyfriend Chris Brown. In an interview with Diane Sawyer, the singer said that, in her opinion, it takes eight or nine incidents of domestic violence before someone leaves an abusive relationship, and then many reenter it.

So why would someone stay in such a situation, and why would they ever return if they'd gotten out? It may seem outrageous, but the dynamic of domestic violence is complicated. Usually, it is because a person feels lonely. That's typically due to the fact that the victims have a lack of confidence and in some cases actually believe that they deserve the beating. In some cases, violence is all they know—they grew up with it, and as adults, they believe it's normal on some level. In many situations of domestic violence, the victim just doesn't know how to get out—in part because leaving an abuser can escalate the violence even more. This may be especially true if a male abuser is someone who touts his masculinity, sees himself as the master of the house, compares himself to other violent offenders in the media, or characterizes the violence of others as justified.

What Corporations Can Do

Too often, some corporations look the other way when it comes to domestic violence. If it doesn't happen in the workplace, at times a few corporate leaders reason, then it's not their concern. But with violence in the home too often impacting the workplace these days, corporate leaders can no longer afford to look the other way. Aside from an offender coming to the job site to contain or control the victim, there can be financial costs to the organization, such as excessive health care costs, excessive absenteeism, lateness, or battered employees being distracted. They may miss work for pending legal proceedings, obtaining medical care, or handling threatening phone calls because the batterer may excessively call or text. Absenteeism and lowered productivity can also happen on the batterer's end as well.

Because of these ramifications, corporations must have a workplace violence prevention policy as well as a domestic violence policy to explain potential company actions. For instance, the company may decide to offer individuals a hotline to counseling or even some form of assistance if an abused employee decides to leave their abuser. This information must be prepared ahead of time, usually in the form of an Employee Assistance Program, and it needs to be available at a moment's notice. Corporations may even, in conjunction with their legal and security teams, prepare some sort of response team to deal with domestic violence.

Other steps organizations can take to proactively assist employees in potentially volatile situations include designating a parking space closer to the building for the employee or hiring uniformed security officers to escort the employee to and from the building. A uniformed security officer or even a couple of supervisors can be effective deterrents. For everyone's safety, however, you should ensure that these escorts are trained in dealing with high-threat individuals so they know what to look for when escorting someone to and from a car. Another option is hiring executive protection, which are higher-paid agents trained to deal with higher levels of threats. Often, these agents are off-duty or retired law enforcement.

If the individual has left the batterer, another helpful measure may be to change the individual's shift schedule or, if possible, move them to a different facility. That may serve to throw off the batterer, making it more difficult for them to locate the individual.

What Can Be Done!

Often, the "straw that breaks the camel's back" is when someone is fired. Even some long-term employees have turned to violence; if a long-term employee starts showing signs of increased absenteeism or increased tardiness, those changes may be indicators of future violent acts. Most high-functioning people won't turn to violence if they're fired, but getting fired may be all it takes to trigger a low-functioning person who has violent tendencies or who was violent in the past. Take Marion Guy Williams for example. Williams, a man described as a loner who was estranged from his family, was fired from Knight Transportation shortly before he shot his former coworker and supervisor Mike Dawid and then himself.

Situations like this are why, as a company leader, you should have measures in place for letting someone go. Those measures should include a neutral manager or even outside security consultants to actually carry out the termination. For instance, during the termination meeting itself, don't allow the employee to take a break; there have been instances where a person took a break, went to their locker, and came back with a gun to shoot the person who was firing them. Lockers can be very dangerous both in the workplace and in schools. In one case, a fellow student saw another student place a gun in his locker. Thank goodness he told school officials. This was a middle school student at Penn Wood. Located in his locker was a 40 caliber. Imagine if you walked this student to his locker in order to gather his belongings before suspension.

If the employee being fired has an issue with a particular supervisor, particularly if this is the reason for termination, then that supervisor should not carry out the termination. If a real potential threat is involved, then there should be more of a presence than an unarmed, uniformed security person; a much higher level of security officer or an executive protection agent should be on-site, blending into the work environment and waiting outside the termination room ready to escort the individual off the property. The escort should maintain respect for the person being terminated; don't walk someone through the middle of the office or work floor followed by two big suits, which can be threatening and undignified.

If an employee is to be notified that he or she is "suspended pending an investigation," this can be done over the phone to reduce the potential for violence. Use phrases such as, "It's been a hard day," "I understand you're having a hard time," "I respect you," "I want you to feel better," combined with telling the person to stay home and they'll be compensated for the day, to reduce potentially volatile situations and keep the potentially dangerous person out of the workplace.

Once a person has been terminated, their last paycheck must be mailed immediately. Don't wait until the next payroll date to pay the person. Have a physical paycheck made out and overnighted to the individual. This action can help eliminate the person's excuse to come back on-site and ask for a last paycheck.

Set boundaries. Give the person a specific phone number and contact for questions, but reinforce the rule that they're not allowed to come back on-site. Again, convey this message in a firm way that allows the individual to retain his or her dignity. The goal is to give the person hope that they're moving on to a better future.

Discussing a severance package is appropriate, if needed. If unemployment is filed, don't contest—at least in cases where having a small amount of income could potentially deter them from coming back to the workplace with ill intent. Make it easy for the person to transition away from the company and reduce the likelihood of their obsessing over the firing. The key is to think outside normal protocol when dealing with someone who is potentially violent.

CHAPTER 5

Substance Abuse

Substance abuse can have a negative impact on conditions in the workplace, from illegal narcotics, such as heroin, cocaine, and methamphetamines, to legal substances, such as alcohol and prescription drugs.

Per the National Council on Alcohol and Drug Dependence (NCADD), alcohol and drug use among employees and their family members can be an expensive problem for business and industry, with issues ranging from lost productivity, absenteeism, injuries, fatalities, theft, and low employee morale, to an increase in health care, legal liabilities, and workers' compensation costs.

NCADD gives the following explanation on drug and alcohol use in the workplace:

> The impact of alcoholism and drug dependence in the workplace often focuses on four major issues:
>
> - premature death/fatal accidents
> - injuries/accident rates
> - absenteeism/extra sick leave
> - loss of production

In addition, family members living with someone's alcoholism or drug use may also suffer significant job performance-related problems—including absenteeism, lack of focus, increased health-related problems, and use of health insurance.

Two specific kinds of drinking behavior significantly contribute to the level of work-performance problems: drinking right before or during working hours (including drinking at lunch and at company functions), and heavy drinking the night before that causes hangovers during work the next day.

And it isn't just alcoholics who can generate problems in the workplace. Research has shown that the majority of alcohol-related work-performance problems are associated with nondependent drinkers who may occasionally drink too much, not exclusively by alcohol-dependent employees.

There is always a level of risk when using any drug, including prescription or over-the-counter medications.

Drug reactions vary from person to person. If an employee is taking a drug he hasn't had before, he won't know how it will affect him. It's important to follow a doctor's advice when taking prescription drugs and to discuss any side effects and how this might impact work.

The effects of prescription drugs such as benzodiazepines (e.g., Xanax) can have an impact on an employee's work and this should be discussed with a doctor. Long-term use in particular may become problematic.

Testing for Substances in the Workplace

As a company leader, it's critical that you have mandatory drug testing written into your policies because tests can help assess whether someone has the potential or the propensity toward violence. You must consult with legal counsel to confirm that any type of testing is legal before you implement a mandatory testing policy. A number of approaches are available to you, but as of this writing, these are the most common. Always check with your legal counsel to confirm what you do is current.

Preemployment testing is often conducted before a person is hired can be extended to include some type of drug testing. Most companies who prescreen for drugs use urine testing, which is cost effective for screening for a range of illicit and prescription drugs. Some employers prefer either an oral fluid (mouth swab) or a hair follicle test, which offer greater security during testing because the collection of the sample can be observed and the window of detection is much longer. The Substance Abuse and Mental Health Services Administration (SAMHSA) guidelines recommend testing for five illicit drugs—amphetamines, THC, cocaine, opiates, and phencyclidine—as well as alcohol. An eight-panel test for these substances adds barbiturates, benzodiazepines, and methaqualone to the list, and a ten-panel test adds methadone and propoxyphene to the list.[21]

Reasonable suspicion testing, also known as probable or for-cause testing, is "conducted when supervisors document observable signs and symptoms that lead them to suspect drug use or a drug-free workplace policy violation." Again, this test is conducted when there is suspected violation of a written policy.

---

21 "Workplace Drug Testing," *elaws – Drug-Free Workplace Advisor*, United States Department of Labor, https://webapps.dol.gov/elaws/asp/drugfree/drugs/dt.asp#q6

Random testing is conducted in the workplace on an unannounced basis on employees whose identifications are selected from a pool of information. This type of testing can serve as a deterrent because employees never know when they'll be required to test.

Return-to-Duty testing is conducted on employees who have previously tested positive and have gone through some form of treatment for substance abuse before returning to work. In some organizations, it's also used on employees who have been absent for a period of time, regardless of the reason.

Each company and state has its own guidelines as to "return to duty" and often this can be found in the HR manual when you begin work. However, as a standard, per the Substance Abuse Professionals—an outline of the following process can be referenced on their website.

What Is the DOT Return-to-Duty Process?

In any public transportation job, a positive test or the refusal to be tested is a violation, as well as a number of other things that are prohibited by the Department of Transportation (DOT).

When an employee has a violation, DOT requires the employer to immediately remove that employee from safety-sensitive functions. An employer who allows an employee with a violation to continue performing safety-sensitive functions is subject to fines, up to $10,000 per day.

An employee who has a violation has two options:

- He/she can find another job, outside of the transportation industry**, or**
- He/she can be considered for returning to safety-sensitive functions in the transportation industry but only after

successfully completing DOT's return-to-duty process and then providing a negative result on a return-to-duty drug and/or alcohol testing.

The return-to-duty process requires involvement of a qualified and trained Substance Abuse Professional (SAP).

The SAP must conduct a face-to-face clinical evaluation of the employee. DOT's rule then *requires* the SAP to recommend treatment and/or education for the employee.

The SAP must send a report to the employer, specifying the SAP's recommendation for treatment and/or education.

The SAP must then monitor the employee's progress in the recommended program of treatment and/or education.

When the SAP determines that the employee has made sufficient progress, the SAP will schedule a follow-up evaluation for the employee.

Based on that evaluation, the SAP will report to the employer that the employee has successfully complied with the SAP's recommendation (or that the employee has *not* complied).

If the SAP reports that the employee has successfully complied with the recommendation, then the employer will decide whether to arrange for a return-to-duty test for the employee. (The employer is not obligated to take the employee back.)

If the SAP reports that the employee has not successfully complied with the recommendation, then the employer cannot return to the employee to safety-sensitive functions.

An employee who has not successfully complied with the SAP's recommendation may not return to safety-sensitive functions for any DOT employer until the SAP's recommendations have been fully met and the employee is able to provide a negative return-to-duty test.

All of these can usually be found in an employee HR handbook, discussed with an HR representative or found on a state sourced website.

Background Checking

The more information you have on an individual that before you hire them, the better, and background checks should also be an essential part of your pre-employment screening, as stated earlier in this book. A background check should include a Social Security trace, which can reveal all the places a person has lived in the past. That allows for more specified background checks in the areas in which the person lived, which involves going to the courthouse and checking records to see if there are any arrests or convictions for past bad acts. Granted, only convictions can affect job offers; a person can't be denied an employment because of past arrests.

The expense involved in conducting background checks and preemployment screenings is nominal compared to the impact on a business from an incident occurring.

If, for example, you're considering hiring a military veteran, it is important to obtain that person's DD Form 214, commonly known as a DD-214. A DD-214 is a resume of sorts that lists the veteran's military duties, rank, job specialty, education, recognitions, and foreign service. It also includes their condition of discharge—honorable, general, other than honorable, dishonorable, or bad conduct.[22] It is important to have access to a veteran's past experiences, not only from an employment qualifications standpoint but also to potentially shed light on a workplace situation if you begin to see signs of post-traumatic stress disorder (PTSD). Information in a

---

22 "Welcome to DD214!" *DD214* website, www.dd214.us/.

DD-214 may help you to assess where a situation may be heading in regards to the potential for violence.

Telephone Assessment

A telephone assessment is needed in cases where there is not a local expert on the ground where the potential harmful person is working. A telephone assessment is effective but, of course, it is always better to see a person face to face. The core areas in assessing are scope, data collection, analysis of policies and procedures, threat analysis, and vulnerability analysis. Identifying the scope is probably the most important step in the process, as it identities what needs to be protected.

That threat assessment expert can get an idea of where this person is in their life by asking direct questions such as:

- What is your outlook on the world?
- How do you characterize yourself in terms of self-esteem?
- Are you suicidal?
- Do you plan on physically injuring anyone?
- Do you own a gun? If so, when did you purchase it?
- What are your hobbies? What do you like to do in your spare time?
- Are you drinking or using drugs?
- Do you spend a lot of time alone? Or are you involved in activities with other people?
- Can you convince me why I should believe what you are saying?

The questions will also explore the person's behavioral controls:

- Are you impulsive?
- Do you anger easily?
- Do you get a lot of stimulation in your life? For instance, are you a daredevil or do you get a thrill out of taking chances?

The assessment also includes scenarios to help determine the individual's level of empathy and impulse control.

What Can Be Done!

Work can be an important and effective place to address alcoholism and other drug issues by establishing or promoting programs focused on improving health. Many individuals and families face a host of difficulties closely associated with problem drinking and drug use, and these problems quite often spill over into the workplace. By encouraging and supporting treatment, employers can dramatically assist in reducing the negative impact of alcoholism and addiction in the workplace, while reducing their costs.

Without question, establishment of an Employee Assistance Program (EAP) is the most effective way to address alcohol and drug problems in the workplace. EAPs deal with all kinds of problems and provide short-term counseling, assessment, and referral of employees with alcohol and drug abuse problems, emotional and mental health problems, marital and family problems, financial problems, dependent care concerns, and other personal problems that can affect the employee's work. This service is confidential. These programs are usually staffed by professional counselors and may be operated in-house with agency personnel, under a contract with other agencies or EAP providers, or a combination of the two. Additionally, employers can address substance use and abuse in their employee population by: implementing drug-free workplace and other written substance abuse policies; offering health benefits that provide comprehensive coverage for substance use disorders, including aftercare and counseling; reducing stigma in the workplace; and educating employees about the health and productivity hazards of substance abuse through company wellness programs. However, when assessing threats in the workplace I recommend a threat assessment consultant, not an EAP clinician.

- Research has demonstrated that alcohol and drug treatment pays for itself in reduced healthcare costs that begin as soon as people begin recovery.
- Employers with successful EAPs and DFWPs report improvements in morale and productivity and decreases in absenteeism, accidents, downtime, turnover, and theft.
- Employers with longstanding programs also report better health status among employees and family members and decreased use of medical benefits by these same groups.

Some facts about alcohol in the workplace:

- Workers with alcohol problems were 2.7 times more likely than workers without drinking problems to have injury-related absences.
- A hospital emergency department study showed that 35 percent of patients with an occupational injury were at-risk drinkers.

- Breathalyzer tests detected alcohol in 16 percent of emergency room patients injured at work.
- Analyses of workplace fatalities showed that at least 11 percent of the victims had been drinking.
- Large federal surveys show that 24 percent of workers report drinking during the workday at least once in the past year.
- One-fifth of workers and managers across a wide range of industries and company sizes report that a coworker's on- or off-the-job drinking jeopardized their own productivity and safety.

Some facts about drugs in the workplace:

- Workers who report having three or more jobs in the previous five years are about twice as likely to be current or past-year users of illegal drugs as those who have had two or fewer jobs, as reported by NCADD.
- Seventy percent of the estimated 14.8 million Americans who use illegal drugs are employed.
- Marijuana is the most commonly used and abused illegal drug by employees, followed by cocaine, with prescription drug use steadily increasing.

In my own experience, when a violent act has taken place, many times alcohol is present, which is why experiences tells me, when assessing a workplace or domestic violence situation, to ask about the person's relationship with alcohol. Alcohol decreases the chemical production of the neurotransmitter serotonin in the brain, which may cause paranoia, violence, anxiety, insomnia, mood swings, and hallucinations. My caution is borne out by the facts. Alcohol abuse is not a predictor of violence—just because someone abuses alcohol doesn't mean that person will inflict harm on another person. But alcohol is the chemical most related to violence, according to American criminologist Marvin Wolfgang, who found that a majority of homicides in Philadelphia involved alcohol.[23]

Scientists and non-scientists alike have recognized the association between alcohol consumption and violent or aggressive behavior. One study found that "up to 86 percent of homicide offenders, 37 percent of assault offenders, 60 percent of sexual offenders, up to 57 percent of men and 27 percent of women involved in marital violence"[24] were drinking at the time of the offense.

According to the National Council on Alcohol and Drug Dependence, "Alcohol is a factor in 40 percent of all violent crimes today," and "alcohol, more than any illegal drug, was found to be closely associated with violent crimes. . . . About three million violent crimes occur each year in which victims perceive the offender to have been drinking and statistics related to alcohol use by violent offenders generally show that about half of all homicides and assaults are committed when the offender, victim, or both have been drinking. Among violent crimes, with the exception of robberies, the offender is far more likely to have been drinking than under the influence of other drugs."[25]

---

23 Martin Wolfgang, "Victim Precipitated Criminal Homicide," *Journal of Criminal Law and Criminology*, 48, no. 1 (1957), http://scholarlycommons.law.northwestern.edu/cgi/viewcontent.cgi?article=4565&context=jclc.

24 "Alcohol Alert," *National Institute on Alcohol Abuse and Alcoholism* no. 38 (1997), http://pubs.niaaa.nih.gov/publications/aa38.htm.

25 "Alcohol, Drugs and Crime," *National Council on Alcoholism and Drug Dependence, Inc.*, www.ncadd.org/about-addiction/alcohol-drugs-and-crime.

While there are many factors, as mentioned, one considered culprit is serotonin, which is a chemical messenger in the brain that is believed to function as a behavioral inhibitor. Decreased serotonin activity is associated with increased impulsivity and aggressiveness. Alcohol and drugs can affect serotonin levels in the body, temporarily elevating serotonin, resulting in feelings of euphoria. Many people continue drinking or taking drugs to try to replicate these feelings of euphoria, which only exacerbates the problem.[26]

When someone's employment is terminated, they may turn to alcohol or drugs for a sense of well-being or to numb their depression or anger at being unemployed. If they are drinkers already, unemployment may lead to an increase in their consumption, which could potentially raise the risk of the person returning to the jobsite.

Alcohol-related behavior should immediately be considered a high risk, but alcohol is not the whole story. If I'm being called in to assess the case, most likely it's not because Joe Smith is a drinker. It's because Joe is maybe a loner or has started missing more work or lately appears to be depressed. Then during the investigation, if Joe is drinking, it will be revealed, which will move him to being assessed as a higher risk assessment versus a low or moderate risk. Utilizing the previously discussed internal threat level scale you've now put in place, it is time to raise the "threat level" for this employee.

Again, it is a combination of factors, like putting together a jigsaw puzzle and understanding how all the individual pieces work together. Once the picture is painted, I make the most accurate threat assessment I can. It is a combination of an art, science, and an experienced expert.

Admittedly, it can be difficult for a supervisor to tell when an employee is starting to have a problem with drugs or alcohol. People,

---

26 Robin Wasserman, "Serotonin Depletion," *Livestrong.com*, May 23, 2016, www.livestrong.com/article/221617-serotonin-depletion/.

in general, are often overwhelmed with the day-to-day routine of work and life, so taking the time to interact one-on-one with workers can be difficult to accomplish. The focus is typically on the bare basics of the tasks that must be accomplished rather than really identifying when someone might be having problems that could result in violence in the workplace.

Then, of course, there is always the mindset that "it's not going to happen here." Even with all the workplace incidents in the news, many company leaders are busy managing their own areas of responsibility, so they don't make the time to take precautions, or in some cases, where the company employs a security or loss prevention director, department managers simply don't place emphasis on security as being within their realm of oversight.

But there are usually pre-indicators if someone is on the lookout for them. That takes training of managers and the general workforce to know what to look for, which means that introducing an educational program like this in your company might be worth considering. Substance abuse—alcohol especially—is easy enough to miss as an indicator of violence because drinking is so socially acceptable. People often meet up after work to have a drink together, so no one points to it as a component of workplace violence. Again, alcohol in and of itself doesn't mean someone is going to be violent, but as a company leader, you should be watchful of changes in an individual and consider whether bringing in a threat assessment expert is warranted, someone that the individual can talk to, even if only for an hour-long phone call so the expert can help reveal whether an individual has a propensity toward violence and determine the next steps. In-person meetings are best, but if this isn't possible, then the phone is a good substitute and an effective assessment tool, especially when time is of the essence.

CHAPTER 6

Weapons Use

One of my cases involved a young man in his twenties who lived with his father and displayed odd behavior of concern to his employer. What is *odd*? Describing odd behavior is not always easy because it is largely a subjective call. What appears to be odd to one person may not be odd to another. For example, if people add tattoos to their bodies and take on a less-than-business-like appearance, they are not likely to be exhibiting odd behavior if they work in a tattoo parlor or a nightclub. However, the same behavior in a financial institution might be reason for concern. If you have a gut feeling, talk about it with your manager and together you can assess it more accurately or bring in a consultant, if there is real concern.

A verbal threat hadn't yet been made, but Jacobs, the manager at a small manufacturing company, had a strong suspicion that one of his workers was teetering on the brink of committing a violent act. His employee appeared to be hopeless and seriously depressed and was medicated. The employee mostly kept to himself, however, he exploded with anger one day and threw a wrench across the floor, almost hitting another employee. As the threat became more likely, Jacobs called us for help. We met with the employee in person off-site and asked him a few questions. It is my opinion that meeting off-site in most circumstances is safer than on-site, unless there is trained security standing nearby.

"Are there any weapons in the house such as firearms?" I asked the employee.

"Well, yes," he answered. "I live with my father, and he owns guns."

This, coupled with his depression and Jacobs's instincts, raised a red flag.

"Are they secured in a locked safe?"

"No," he answered. "He just keeps them in his room."

I asked the man if his father would be willing to remove the weapons from the home or buy a safe to secure them in, which the father did. After the employee completed and passed a threat assessment and a fitness-for-duty, he returned to work. There were no drugs involved or alcohol, and he agreed to see a psychiatrist on a weekly basis.

Jacobs was right when he raised the alarm. There is a significantly increased risk of fatality if a weapon is used in a violent encounter. The concern in a situation like this is the immediate threat of homicide and/or suicide. If a person in this frame of mind had a drinking problem, then having an easily accessible weapon during a difficult time could increase the threat level. As with the other threats, the use of weapons by an individual does not, by itself, create a violent situation. There are many responsible weapon users who are peaceful and nonviolent.

As a gun owner and security expert, I believe in the Second Amendment's right to bear arms. However, it is important to recognize that this entitlement comes with responsibility, and I don't believe the right to bear arms should extend to men and women with questionable psychological profiles that place them at high risk for homicide and/or suicide.

If, however, a person suspected of meeting this psychological profile is brought to our attention, we look at the person's background with weapons to make an assessment: Are they a hunter? Do they live in an open-carry state? Are guns a lifelong interest or did they just recently buy a gun, maybe saying that it's for home protection?

On the threat assessment scale, having firearms in the home or being a lifelong hunter actually places this person at low risk, unless a number of other components are involved, such as drinking or depression. However, the threat level moves toward moderate risk if the individual carries a firearm in their vehicle, if they have recently increased their frequency of visits to the firearm range, or if they are emotionally stimulated by talk of guns. It becomes high when an individual inappropriately displays a firearm or develops a preoccupation with guns, weapons, and violence. A person who talks about weapons at inappropriate times is likely using them to make veiled threats or manipulate situations.

In a disturbing and sad example as recent as July 2016, a mother had called a family meeting with her husband and daughters. When they gathered to meet, the mother pulled out her firearm and shot both her daughters. The husband and girls tried to run and made it out into the street. The mother followed them, fired more shots, and then even went back into her home to reload her weapon. Police made it onto the scene and after repeated attempts to get the mother to drop her weapon, had to open fire.

This was a woman who worked as a receptionist and had shown no warning signs that were apparent to the family but who was in the midst of a separation from her husband. Having a weapon at home, when tensions are high, can unfortunately leave people to act out of the ordinary, not thinking of the final consequences.

If you own a gun, keep your firearm securely stowed in a safe to help keep it from ending up in criminal hands or even in your hands if there are emotional situations at hand.

While many have firearms as a form of home-invasion protection, often they are not prepared to use them, not properly trained, and can often end up having the weapon used against them.

Sometimes having to go through the process of retrieving a firearm rather than just having it ready to grab and go can be the difference between a family spat—and an entire family dead.

Needless to say, if children are in the house, it is absolutely essential that you have your weapon secured. We've heard so many stories about young siblings shooting each other. Recently, a gun advocate who spent a tremendous amount of time on social media touting her gun collection had her own child shoot her from the back seat of the car. Why she would have her weapon unsecured with a toddler in a car leaves many questions, particularly about her parenting style. There are several affordable options, including keypads and fingerprint accessible safes that can be purchased with ease from Amazon or Costco. These types of safes will prevent those not trained, nor of age from gaining access. The life you save could be your own in this instance.

Being prepared is important. As a former police officer and the CEO of a security company, I myself have a firearm easily accessible; however, I do not have young children currently living in my home. I lock it away whenever there is company. I am also properly trained in using the weapon in both self-defense situations and proactive scenarios, which leads me to discuss what some refer to as the "parking lot controversy."

The Parking Lot Controversy

Firearms laws vary from state to state and many are not without controversy. If your place of business is in an open-carry state, it will be hard for you to contain guns in the workplace. Some states, including Oklahoma, have language in their state constitution stating that employers are immune from damages resulting from the use of weapons retrieved from parking areas.

As of 2015, more than eighteen states have laws that allow an employee to store a firearm in his or her vehicle in the company's parking lot, according to the San Francisco-based gun control advocacy group Law Center to Prevent Gun Violence.[27] If you are in one of these states, then you can keep firearms out of the offices and off factory floors but not out of the parking lot. While this makes it harder for you to enforce gun-free zones, it makes it easier for a disgruntled employee to retrieve a firearm from the parking lot and return to the workplace to create havoc. Many companies reason that parking lots are private property and should also be bound to the gun-free zone, otherwise the law is akin to allowing guests into your home with a gun. This creates a conflict for you as a company leader in one of these states: on the one hand, you don't want to violate a person's rights by disallowing open carry, but on the other hand, you need to protect your employees. Establishing a gun-free workplace policy for everyone can reduce incidents of homicide in the workplace. But to do this, you to need to know your state laws.

Whenever possible, you should have written policies prohibiting firearms in the workplace. These policies should be drafted with the help of an attorney, and they must be made known and be

27 Peyton Smith, "Providing a Safe Workplace When Employees Are Licensed to Carry," *Reed & Scardino* website (blog), October 16, 2015, http://reedscardino.com/providing-a-safe-workplace-when-employees-are-licensed-to-carry/.

enforced for all employees, visitors, and subcontractors. You can, like many companies in open-carry states, post "No Guns" signs in the entryways as a form of self-enforcement. In this way, they're letting people know the preference for on-site carry laws without strictly enforcing their policy.

Even though state law may indemnify employers from damages resulting from the use of weapons retrieved from parking areas, there always exists a level of liability for the company. To offset your risk, you can use Crime Prevention Through Environmental Design (CPTED), which involves making engineering and administrative changes with safety in mind during the construction or renovation of facilities. CPTED designs changes include increased lighting, eliminating escape routes, or enhancing visibility around your building's exterior.

In the beginning, CPTED looked like this:

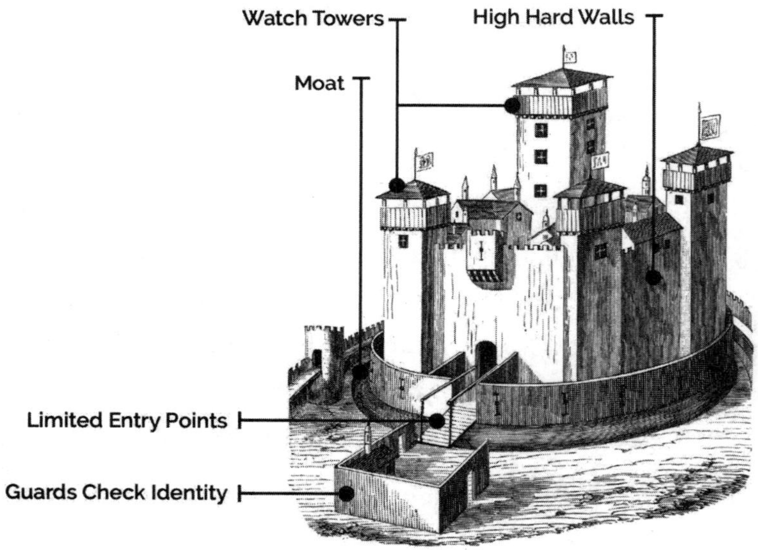

Now, it looks like this:

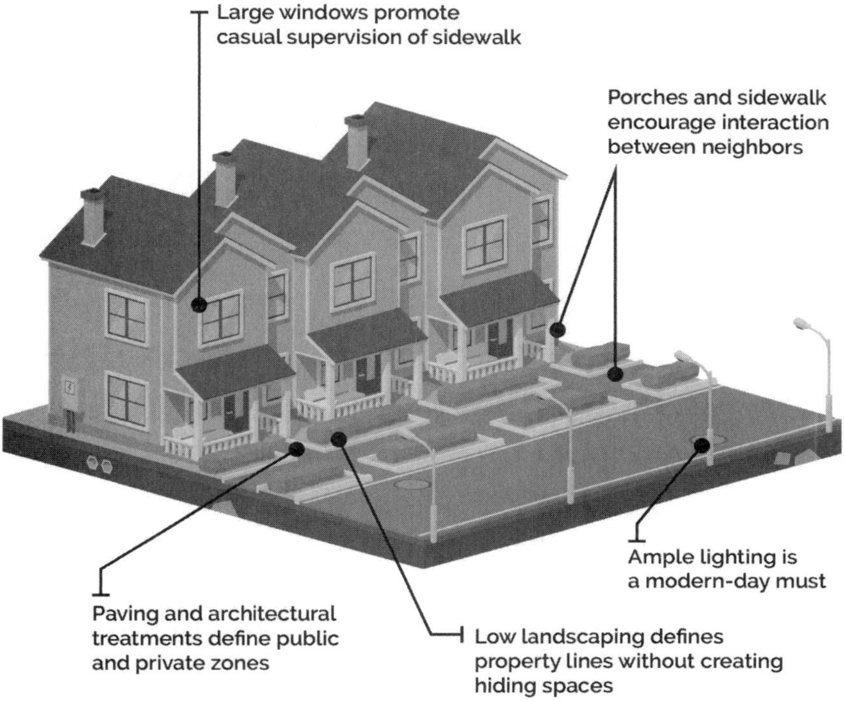
Large windows promote
casual supervision of sidewalk
Porches and sidewalk
encourage interaction
between neighbors
Ample lighting is
a modern-day must
Paving and architectural
treatments define public
and private zones
Low landscaping defines
property lines without creating
hiding spaces

Example of CPTED for both personal and business needs.

Defusing Situations & Intuition

If you were driving to work and saw a car ahead of you beginning to swerve, you would probably brake lightly to widen the space between you and the other driver in an effort to avoid an accident. Your gut and observation skills kept you on your toes and ready to plunge into action if needed.

The same goes for mitigating potential violence in the workplace. Employee training can help your employees recognize and manage potentially violent people on the job, whether they be other employees, clients, or strangers. Training can also help employees at all levels understand how to defuse situations that don't involve an active shooter.

When a person is in the stage of rage, he or she may jump from one point to another, often not wanting to hear what you are saying. The broken-record technique can often be effective in these situations. Just repeat—calmly and assertively—what you want to say. For example, "John didn't mean to speak abruptly to you. I know you are angry and I know we can work through this." You can also make a negative assertion, which often stops an argument right away by you appearing to agree with what is being said. "You are right. I was wrong and I see it from your point of view."

Teach employees to seek guidance from their own internal resources and to listen to their gut. To paraphrase the concepts first laid down by Albert Einstein, the intuitive mind is a sacred gift, and the rational mind is a faithful servant: we have created a society that honors the servant and has forgotten the gift. Ask yourself questions and listen to the first answer that pops into your mind. Keep an intuition journal. Your intuition is that moment in time that you pay attention to a small, persistent thought. One of my favorite TV shows is *NCIS*, and the main character, Gibbs, is known for his intuition, or "trusting his gut." This theory on intuition helping you make better decisions gets more concrete when you follow the work of Helen Fisher. According to Fisher, there is a brain process called "chunking." Over time, your brain chunks and links more and more patterns together, then stores these clusters of knowledge in your long-term memory. So when you see a tiny detail of a familiar design, you instantly recognize the larger composition—and that's what we regard as a flash of intuition and trusting your gut. Intuition is a powerful tool that people use on a daily basis to guard and protect themselves and others in certain aspects of their lives.

If you encounter an angry person, you may sense if they are liable to explode into rage. Your gut may tell you that something is amiss; you may see the person begin to pace back and forth nervously. What do you do?

First, you must deal with hostility by redirecting it so that it does not get a hold on you. The person is likely not upset with you specifically, so your first response should not be defensive. Defuse the encounter by using various learned distraction techniques. Being defensive in the past helped us to survive. Knee-jerk defensive reactions can be good but usually only if we have to dodge a steam engine or a baseball flying at our face.

Unfortunately, through faulty learning we start to flee what could actually be good for us. You can build confidence when you relax with other people who have their own perspectives. Think about times you were overly defensive and your response was not necessary. Close your eyes and think of yourself responding differently, more evenly. Real strength is when we can put our swords down and risk being open. By doing this, we can defuse the other person and deflect his or her anger before it reaches a boiling point.

First, if possible, get help before trouble starts from a supervisor, coworker, or police officer. Use a prearranged warning signal to alert others.

Second, establish an appropriate tone:

- Stay calm. Your tone will help keep the person calm.
- Talk slowly and calmly. Use a firm, confident tone.
- Don't threaten, but inform of consequences of inappropriate behavior.

Third, speak to the person in a non-confrontational way:

- Criticize the issue or behavior, not the person. By dealing with the issue or the behavior, you avoid attacking the other person. "Your behavior at this moment is not tolerated. I believe in you and your potential, but at this moment the way you are interacting with others is not appropriate."
- Stand at a forty-five-degree angle to add space between you and the angered person. Do not square off.
- Avoid absolutes—right/wrong, bad/good. Phrases like "you always" or "you never" are absolutes that impede communication.
- Send "I feel" messages instead of "you" messages that lay blame on the other person. For example, instead of saying, "You don't know what you're talking about," say, "I don't understand what you're trying to say." This is an "I" message, which assumes some personal responsibility.

Fourth, communicate respect to de-escalate hostility:

- Use the appropriate listening skills and nonaggressive body language. Face the person and maintain eye contact, but not in an intimidating fashion. Be attentive and relaxed, keep an open mind, listen to their words, and don't interrupt. Do not impose your solutions. You also need to observe physical and behavioral changes, such as sweating, loud speech, clenched teeth, finger pointing, standing too close, rapid breathing, an aggressive posture, or restlessness. Stop talking and really listen, put the other person at ease, remove distractions, empathize, be patient, avoid personal prejudice, and listen to the tone of his or her voice. Do not move toward the person, as this will escalate them.

Again, stand at a forty-five-degree angle to open up the space between you and them.

- Show an interest in resolving the issue or meeting the other person's needs and concerns.
- Acknowledge the importance of the other person's concern.
- Refrain from openly judging his or her behavior.

If you become angry or fear for your safety, be prepared to disengage:

- Try to identify an escape route at the beginning of the encounter.
- Seek safety at your first opportunity. Explain the need for a break or time-out. Make a commitment (you or someone else) to return to the matter. Offer food or a beverage, if available and appropriate.

Finally, after your encounter, debrief your experience with someone you trust.

Bomb Detection

Threatening weapons come in many forms. If you receive a suspicious letter or package, assess the package before proceeding further.

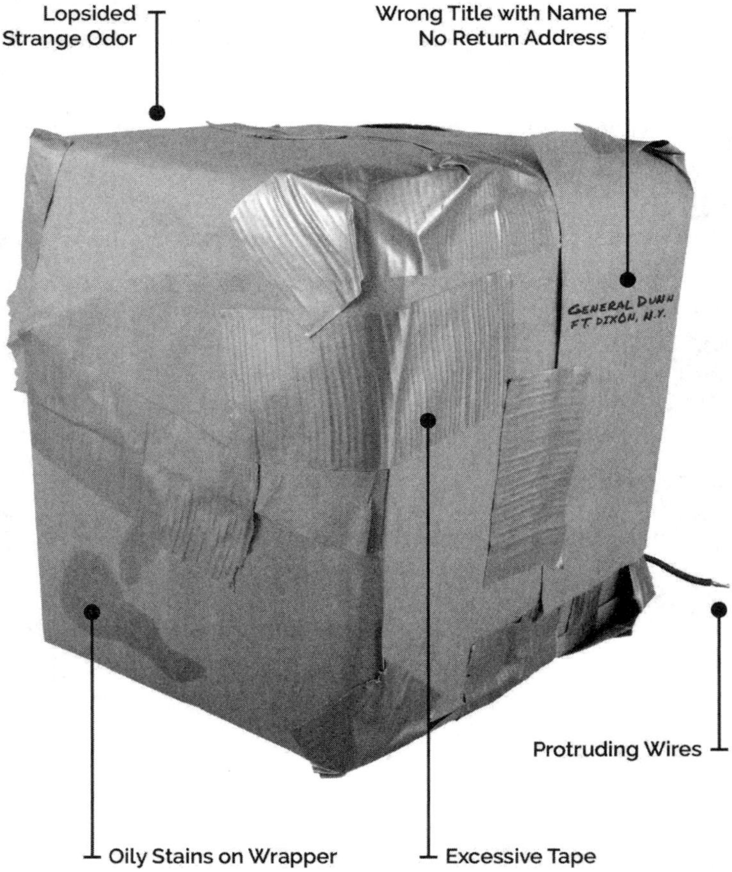

Traits of a suspicious package include:

- no return address
- protruding wires
- wrong title with name
- oily stains on wrapping
- strange odor
- excessive postage
- misspelled words
- lopsided shape

Take these steps when dealing with a suspicious package:

1. Handle with care. Don't shake or bump the package. In fact, it's best not to touch the suspected package or letter any more than necessary.
2. Don't use a cell phone or activate a fire alarm; either of these could detonate a package. Use a hard-wired phone to call the police.
3. Clear the area.

What Can Be Done! Active Shooter

In 2012, a mass shooting occurred in a Century 16 movie theater in Aurora, CO. As the movie *Dark Knight Rises* played, a lone gunman dressed in tactical clothing set off teargas grenades and shot into the audience. Twelve people were killed and seventy others were injured. James Eagan Holmes was arrested in his car outside of the cinema shortly afterward. He had no known criminal record and provided no motive or reasoning for his actions. When an active shooter is on the premises, there are a number of options available to you. While there are numerous experts providing some excellent ways in which to respond to these situations, one of the most common and referenced forms is expressed in the video *Run. Hide. Fight. Surviving an Active Shooter Event* by Ready Houston.[28] Here are three options, along with some personal insights for you to consider.

- **Run**. Employ this option only if you're sure your path out of the building is clear.
- **Hide**. This is not always the best option, because sometimes the shooter will seek out people hiding under desks, which is what occurred in the California 101 incident I discussed earlier in the book.
- **Fight**. If you and a group of coworkers can surprise the attacker, this option may prove to be fruitful. However, if you're not feeling well or don't have an advantageous situation, fighting may not be the best option.

However, Run. Hide. Fight. may not always be ideal.

28 *Run. Hide. Fight. Surviving an Active Shooter Event*, July 23, 2012 (City of Houston).

At the time of this writing, the October 1, 2017 Las Vegas Strip shooting is the deadliest mass shooting in United States history. The shooter, sixty-four-year-old Stephen Paddock, had smashed out two windows from a thirty-second-floor suite of the Mandalay Bay Hotel, and opened fire on concertgoers at a country music festival. Fifty-eight people were killed and over 450 were wounded. The shooting lasted eleven minutes before he killed himself as SWAT officers breached the room.

In this situation, the Run. Hide. Fight. method couldn't effectively protect the concertgoers, as the shooter was so elevated. Amidst the panic, confusion, and inability to locate the shooter, concertgoers only had two options: run, or lay flat on the ground.

Whenever you are in a large area full of people, like a concert venue or a sporting event, always have a plan and be aware of your surroundings. It is critical to be able to locate exits and visualize escape strategies should the need arise. I'm not suggesting paranoia—that's not what this book is about. I'm only suggesting that you take thirty seconds to analyze your surroundings before going on to enjoy your event. If you're constantly aware of your surroundings and have a gameplan for the unpredictable, then you will be able to better keep calm should the situation arise.

CHAPTER 7

Hopelessness—The Risks for Self-Harm and Violence

A few years ago, I knew a woman I will call Patricia, who had been born in another country. As a child, she had been molested for many years by a stepparent. She came to Los Angeles in her late teens, but the effect of the abuse followed her. She tried therapy. She tried different kinds of psychotropic medications and antidepressants. Unfortunately, nothing ever really seemed to work. She slept all day; it was easier to sleep than have to get up and get active.

During her college years, she started to self-mutilate by cutting herself. It was as if she wanted to feel something because she felt so numb. In her hopelessness, the pain gave her some kind of feeling. This is an extreme example, after all; there are many people who feel hopeless and don't self-mutilate. Nevertheless, Patricia's story is more common than you might think.

When Patricia reached her breaking point, she would wander the city for days, walking all day and all night. It rained, but she kept walking. When she got tired, she would sit awhile but then continue to walk aimlessly through one California city after another.

She eventually tried many different types of therapists and psychiatrists, and her walking compulsion passed, but nothing really worked to alleviate her feelings completely. She couldn't get to sleep at night and began sleeping until mid-afternoon every day. She became a high-functioning person with major depression, but she was completely lacking in energy or the skills to be in a healthy relationship.

What changed her life was having children. She started having children to relieve her own pain. She would be with men to have a child, and then within a short time period she was gone.

Patricia's experience paints a picture of hopelessness. She never thought she could rid herself of her past and have a healthy relationship. Not everyone who is hopeless becomes a murderer or perpetrates workplace violence or turns to terrorism. There are different levels of hopelessness. The question becomes: at what point does someone who's in a hopeless state, whether suicidal or homicidal, take that next step? If they're suicidal, what makes them not want to kill somebody else?

Hopelessness and Violence

There is little research on the hopelessness of individuals, and it may be something that we'll never truly understand. Again, not everyone who's depressed or hopeless is going to be a murderer, just as not everyone who has a problem with alcohol or drugs will become violent and abusive.

Hopeless people are, however, tortured souls. Their inner dialogue is filled with degrading and derisive content to self and others, and when an individual feels hopeless, the probability of violence will increase. However, the combination of alcohol, drugs, and hopelessness doesn't mean we can look at someone and say, "Oh.

We've got to be careful. You know they're trouble. They're going to be a killer."

Statistics do show that a lot of violent crime and murders happen while under the influence, but just because someone is an alcoholic or suffers from alcoholism doesn't mean they're going to become a murderer. Nevertheless, as we discussed in chapter 5, the presence of these destabilizers does show us that there is something going on that we should pay attention to before it leads to something more serious. We have to look at the same indicators to determine whether someone may be suicidal or homicidal.

Indicators of Potential Violence

Many people in corporations think that a person with suicidal ideations is not a risk for being homicidal. That just isn't true. One of the points that I drive home with my clients is that when someone is suicidal, we need to take the same precautions as we would with someone who may be homicidal. Suicide can very easily and quickly turn into homicidal ideations. It doesn't mean that it's going to happen, of course; it just means you don't want to let your guard down.

Some clients will just send a suicidal employee to an employee assistance program (EAP), or they'll tell them they need to have a fitness-for-duty test. But one of the things they often overlook, and shouldn't, is the need to be very specific when making sure that not only is the person not a threat to themselves, but that they are not a threat to others.

Often, corporate leaders call the police when faced with a suspected suicidal employee. The police then interview the person to determine whether they think the person is a threat to themself or others, but it's easy for a person to bluff their way through this type of suicide evaluation. They may say something like, "No, I was just kidding," or, "Yes, I was sad. I was depressed, but at this moment, no, of course I don't want to hurt myself. I don't want to hurt anybody else." Just like that, they can avoid being taken in for a mental evaluation.

If, however, the police suspect the person is a threat to themselves or others, they can take them in under article 5150 of the Welfare and Institutions Code (WIC) and hold them for seventy-two hours for evaluation. In some cases, that time limit can be extended to two weeks.

A threat assessment expert may also be needed to determine, through a combination of science, intuition, and research, if the individual is a high-, moderate-, or low-risk suicidal threat.

If someone is hopeless, I'm more likely to put him or her on the higher end of the continuum. Hopelessness doesn't extend just to workplace violence; it is key with terrorism as well. Modern suicide bombers aim at causing devastating physical damage. That's their plan of attack, and it's implemented through suicide, such as blowing up planes in midair, strapping bombs to their chest, or driving a truck through a crowded street festival. Terrorists have become very creative at keeping people in fear, to the point that we become afraid to go out because we don't know where violence is going to come from.

There is a sense of hopelessness with the suicide bombers, too, usually because they have been told there is no hope for their life. Some say they are not suicidal but carrying out glorious martyrdom operations. Whatever your belief, hopelessness is part of their psyche, whether it is from mental illness or the hopeless belief that death is the only way they can save themselves and their ideology. It is key to suicidal people in order to defuse the human "bomb," so to speak.

In my assessment, I ask questions such as, "How do you feel about tomorrow? Is there a tomorrow? Do you have any future plans?" If someone answers, "No," it means they can't even think past that moment. That concerns me. They could also be so angry that they can't look at tomorrow.

For example, if you're going to be terminated from your job, how are you going to move from this moment in time to being a little bit more hopeful about tomorrow? Maybe a better job will come about. Maybe this job wasn't even meant to be yours. Maybe you weren't even happy here. It is possible that moving from this job to something potentially much better for you will be the best thing that ever happened. But this requires a glass-half-full versus half-empty perspective.

Hopelessness becomes apparent when there's a loss of interest or pleasure in life. If they're excited about something, maybe their children for instance, that gives me a little bit of hope because I know it's not as serious as it may appear. I also look at appetite or weight changes. Have they gained weight? Have they lost weight? If you've ever gone to the doctor for a visit, they record your weight not only for physical health reasons, but because it can also be a sign of depression. I'm not only going to ask the individual, I'm going to ask the people around them, their supervisors, their managers, their coworkers. I also ask if the person has talked about any kind of sleep deprivation.

In Patricia's case, she was molested at age nine years old and was still dealing with the trauma it left on her. That trauma manifested itself as a sleep disorder. She wanted to sleep because she didn't want to deal with the world, and so it's a lot easier to sleep it off.

When I do an assessment, I don't go right to the person. I try to gather information from their employment files, background checks, running criminal background checks, and their direct supervisors to get some type of picture of who I'm dealing with. Then I'll go talk to the person.

I don't take anything lightly. I'm very specific because you need to ask direct questions in order to get direct answers. I'll ask, "Are you suicidal? Are you homicidal? Have you had any thoughts of hurting yourself or hurting someone else?" I observe if they're agitated. I ask if their energy decreased, perhaps due to feelings of worthlessness or guilty, or in the case of a molestation, a sense of shame.

Some people may be afraid to ask, "Do you want to kill yourself? Do you want to kill someone else?" but you need to ask those things in order to get a good sense of where they are in terms of hope or hopelessness. These questions become very important in identifying the different types of hopelessness and how to overcome them.

The Nine Types of Hopelessness

In their book, *Hope in the Age of Anxiety*, psychology professors Anthony Scioli and Henry Biller discuss hope from a variety of different perspectives, combining psychology with philosophy, biology, anthropology, and even the literary classics.[29] Let's take a closer look at the different types of hopelessness that exist, their causes, and how we can overcome them.

---

29 Anthony Scioli and Henry B. Biller, *Hope in the Age of Anxiety: A Guide to Understanding and Strengthening Our Most Important Virtue* (Oxford, UK: Oxford University Press, 2009.)

THE NINE TYPES OF HOPELESSNESS

1 **Alienation** (Attachment)	2 **Forsakenness** (Attachement & Survival)	3 **Uninspired** (Attachement & Mastery)
4 **Powerlessness** (Mastery)	5 **Oppression** (Mastery & Attachment)	6 **Limitedness** (Mastery & Survival)
7 **Doom** (Survival)	8 **Captivity** (Survival & Attachement)	9 **Helplessness** (Survival & Mastery)

1. Alienation (Attachment)

Alienation may be one of the most frequent forms of hopelessness. Most of us feel "different" in some way, but when that feeling begins to impair our functioning, it is a more serious problem. Not only do alienated individuals believe that they are somehow different, but they also feel as if they have been cut loose from society and are no longer deemed worthy of love, care, or support. In turn, the alienated tend to close themselves off, fearing further pain and rejection.

2. Forsakenness (Attachment and Survival)

The word *forsaken* refers to an experience of total abandonment that leaves individuals feeling alone in their time of greatest need. Recall Job in the Old Testament, crumpled and covered with sores, pleading with a seemingly indifferent god.

3. Uninspired (Attachment and Mastery)

Feeling uninspired can be especially difficult for members of underprivileged minorities, for whom opportunities for growth and positive role models within the group may be either lacking or undervalued.

4. Powerlessness (Mastery)

Individuals of every age need to believe that they can author the story of their life. When that need is thwarted, when one feels incapable of navigating one's way toward desired goals, a feeling of powerlessness can set in.

5. Oppression (Mastery and Attachment)

Oppression involves the subjugation of a person or group. The word *oppressed* comes from the Latin word for "press down," and its synonym, *down-trodden*, suggests a sense of being "crushed under" or "flattened."

6. Limitedness (Mastery and Survival)

When the struggle for survival is combined with a sense of failed mastery, individuals feel limited. They experience themselves as deficient, lacking in the right stuff to make it in the world. This form of hopelessness is all too common among the poor as well as those struggling with severe physical handicaps or crippling learning disabilities.

7. Doom (Survival)

Individuals weighed down by this form of despair presume that their life is over, that their death is imminent. The ones most vulnerable to sinking into this particular circle of hell are those diagnosed with a serious, life-threatening illness, as well as those who see themselves worn out by age or infirmity. Such individuals feel doomed, trapped in a fog of irreversible decline.

8. Captivity (Survival and Attachment)

Two forms of hopelessness can result from captivity. The first consists of physical or emotional captivity enforced by an individual or a group. Prisoners fall into this category as well as those help captive in a controlling, abusive relationship. We refer to this as "other-imprisonment." An equally insidious form of entrapment is "self-imprisonment." This occurs when individuals cannot leave a bad relationship, because their sense of self will not allow it.

9. Helplessness (Survival and Mastery)

Helpless individuals no longer believe that they can live safely in the world. They feel exposed and vulnerable, like a cat after being declawed or a bird grounded by a broken wing. Trauma or repeated exposure to uncontrolled stressors can produce an ingrained sense of helplessness. In the words of one trauma survivor, "I was terrified to go anywhere on my own. I felt so defenseless and afraid that I just stopped doing anything."

Understanding and knowing that there is hope is the most important attribute we can "hope" for in this new day and age. Without hope, we are simply not human.

Contributing to Hopelessness

Corporate leaders should always ask themselves whether the company is contributing to a sense of hopelessness. How are they treating people? How is the environment, the workload, the workforce treating people? We can trigger a person to move and jump off the proverbial cliff without even thinking about it. We need to ask one simple question daily: Are we treating people with respect?

"Respect" is a very important word because, even with terrorism or riots, it raises the point of how things have gotten to where they are today. Somewhere back in time, it is likely that respect was not shown to the perpetrator of violence. Not that it justifies violence or riots or terrorism, but I believe that every one of us has a part in this. How are we treating that employee in the workplace? How do we interact with them? How do others interact with them? How do they interact with us? What's making them escalate to the point of wanting to hurt someone?

Usually, there is a catalyst for some types of violence. Something is a trigger, and the person really becomes hopeless. Bullying is an example of this. A lot of times, teenage killers who went on a school rampage were bullied. So we have to ask: What is our part in this?

That's a tough question to ask, and so we often blame the person instead. We blame the terrorist. We blame the teenager who just killed someone. We blame the enraged worker or commuter or the traumatized veteran quietly suffering alone. We might even blame the person who killed themselves. No one should resort to violence, but we do need to look at ourselves and ask whether we're doing something that contributes to breaking souls and pushing them to be violent. Some of these broken souls only know one way to regain power, and that's by saying, "Look at me. Hear me. See me. If I have to kill ten people in order for you to hear that I'm alive, then I'll do it."

After 9/11, we remembered respect. Everybody had an American flag on their car. There was unity across much of the world, across races, nationalities, and religion. At home, people were saying, "It's okay if you cut me off in line. It's okay if you cut me off on the road. We're Americans. We're bonded." Then, four weeks passed, eight weeks passed, and we were all back to screaming and yelling at each other.

It seems that everyone is so stressed and so focused on their own lives that we're just not able to focus on other people. And this is where problems start. We should always remember the importance of respect. We should always look at how we treat people.

Without hope, violent people can more easily control our lives by keeping us in a constant state of fear.

The Role of Hope

In order to provide hope, we have to dissect where the problem is coming from. If it is terrorism, where is it coming from? We have to go back in time to see how this began if we are to know how to heal it. Why do we need to heal it? Because bigger planes or bigger bombs or better soldiers are not going to stop it. We have to go back to the cause.

Riots often emerge from poverty and injustice. Again, we need to look at how we are treating people and what can be done to remedy it.

In the workplace we have to ask, "What is the cause of this person's propensities? Is it mental illness? Is it alcohol?" If we can restore a person's sense of hope and self-respect, then many times we can prevent a violent act from ever occurring.

Training for Hope

For corporate leaders who suspect potential workplace violence, implementing training is important. My guard force for instance is several hundred strong. In order to make them the best they can be, I need to train them. To train them, I need to put money into them. Employee training is worth the investment. A couple of decades ago, stress management was a big thing, and then all of a sudden it fell off. It was a fad at the time, but it should be much more. We still should be emphasizing stress management, just as we should be putting money into training people in respect, risk assessment, and communication skills

Everything comes down to training, whether it be looking into workplace violence or understanding how to talk to each other, or how to defuse dangerous situations. Making a person a manager or supervisor without training them on how to deal with human behavior could be a ticking time bomb. For some, it's innate, part of who they are, but others need to be taught these skills.

Training Strategies

Because of the importance of learning how to interact with people respectfully, I offer training on respect, listening, and empathy. The more intuitive a corporate leader is with the people who work for that company, the easier it will be to keep anything horrible from happening. This is because they will be in tune with their people. That's not easy to do. Most people are not that intuitive, and others are just too busy with their own lives.

Because training strategies are so important, I have developed different strategies tailored to different situations. For instance, my **Best Model Program** takes people through training modules that involve playing vignettes in a very realistic, but simulated environment. Here, the business can experience and evaluate the psychological and emotional elements that are present in stressful workplace encounters, including the fight-or-flight response. I want people to feel the stress of what it would be like in the situation we're training them for, perhaps defusing a threat or escaping from a violent encounter or even stopping one. Once they get into the simulation and learn, they will likely be able to roll that approach in a real-life situation.

Another effective program is my **Target Program**. With this model, the objectives are terrorism and violent behavior, awareness and assessment, potential threat. It focuses on preparing participants physically and mentally to handle different situations by giving them an understanding of what to look for in a given situation.

My **Global Link Program** is designed to cultivate communication, help express openness, and communicate effectively, while my **Cultural Understanding and Openness Program** takes it a step further and explores culture-related issues and communication styles. In the new global workplace, there are many different types of people that leaders are charged with managing. Managers and workers often find themselves working with people from various countries and backgrounds, and some type of cultural awareness is needed as a result. If you are culturally aware, you can help defuse a potentially violent misunderstanding.

For example, I recently attended a work party for a company with a high percentage of Filipinos. Many of the Filipinos got together to coordinate a customary meal called *dinuguan*. Dinuguan is pork, prepared by roasting the whole pig with an apple in its mouth. When it was delivered, somebody who was non-Filipino made the comment: "This is disgusting. You might as well kill a dog and put an apple in its mouth. It's the same thing."

The comment sparked a huge argument that escalated and wound up being waged largely on social media.

I was brought in to intervene. I spoke to the person who made the comment, saying, "You know, you have to respect other people's cultures. Comparing it to killing and eating a dog is a little extreme."

Some people would have been defensive, but this individual was evolved enough to say they were wrong. "I still feel that way," the employee said, "but I should not have expressed myself out loud and insulted another culture."

It doesn't take much, especially when people are mature and respectful. But it's incredibly important to talk to people and explain to them about cultural differences so we don't say stupid things and trigger an otherwise avoidable confrontation.

What Can Be Done!

When it comes to recognizing and dealing with hopelessness, training is important. Every organization should have some type of EAP program. That's key. You need to be able to give phone numbers to somebody who needs help. You can't force people to call unless it's a fitness-for-duty issue, but if you feel someone is getting to the point where they're a harm to self or others, then you can actually force an employee to have a fitness-for-duty assessment before they can return to work. Always consult legal counsel before you implement a fitness-for-duty.

You also need to have a resource guide for suicide hotlines and domestic violence hotlines in your particular area. There may be national hotlines available if there are no local agencies in your area.

In the event of a suicide or other traumatic event that affects the workplace, you need to have a mental health consultant available to workers. For someone you suspect is suicidal or being abused, you need to have someone do an intervention, and you should have that person on your list so you don't have to think about it if or when a situation arises. These are things you should on hand in the workplace at all times, just in case.

If you have a concern for an employee that seems to be showing suicidal tendencies or signs of deep depression, you might feel uncertain as to how to approach them, or if you should even say anything at all.

First, remember that it is not your job to solve their problems, but you can be an advocate or an open ear for them so they don't feel alone in their struggle.

Don't be afraid to ask directly if they are considering suicide. Asking the question does not increase their potential to act; if anything, it may help to open a dialogue and help you understand where they are in their depression or hopelessness.

Next, be reassuring. Acknowledge that life's journey is difficult and that you understand that speaking about it can be difficult but that you are there for them. Be reassuring that you care about them and their issues.

If they open up, thank them for being honest with you. This opens a mutual respect and reminds the person that they haven't pushed you away with their honesty but rather found someone they can continue to be honest with.

Most importantly, listen. After you have taken the time to really listen, you should suggest they seek support. If you feel comfortable, then you can offer your own situation where you found support helpful in your life. Support recommendations don't just have to include psychological programs. They can also be upcoming events you'd like them to participate in or groups that may get together in a field of interest to them.

And finally, keep in touch. This is as important as the initial listening. Don't ask and then ignore. Follow up, check in with them, and continue to show your genuine concern. See if they need time off or if they're handling their work okay. If they tell you they have immediate plans to commit suicide, however, then this is the time to take further interceptive actions that are approved by your HR team.

When addressing someone you suspect may be suicidal or depressed, it's best to use simple, direct questions, such as:

- What can I do to support you?
- What should I do if I notice your behavior changing?
- How comfortable are you with my checking up/in with you? (Suggest alternative amounts of time.)
- Do you need any changes here at work, schedule-wise or tasks and responsibilities, that we can help alleviate while you work on getting better?

You should also be aware of federal and local laws concerning an employee's mental and physical health. If someone has returned to work after a suicide attempt you may be required to offer them:

- flexible work hours, allowing for personal time off to make medical appointments
- a shift change or location alternative
- reduced hours and/or workload

Lastly, remind them of the confidentiality of your discussion with them. While it is important to keep your team in the loop as to why a worker's performance may be changing, you may not talk about the conversation unless the worker gives you permission to do so. You can remind them of confidentiality, however, if you feel they are a danger to self or others you will have to alert the appropriate individuals to reach out and keep all safe. You need to remind the person that if at any time you feel there is risk involved, you will reach out to get them help. However, it is quite different if the person is either actively suicidal or homicidal.

Provide resources to them such as a crisis hotline, a suicide callback service number, and/or websites that can provide them with more information.

CHAPTER 8

Identification with Perpetrators and Acts of Violence

After an instance of violence on the news, I get an influx of calls that there are more issues at the workplace. So when I'm consulting after any type of media frenzy over any type of violence—whether it be terrorism, workplace violence, school violence, or something else—I always say, "You need to pay extra attention to what's going on in your environment right now, because the more that it is publicized in the media, the more likely it is that something is going to happen again. There's going to be a second one or third one. It's not an isolated case."

This is because people who have a propensity toward violence or are identifying with the perpetrators on the news are more likely to go out and commit an act of violence shortly thereafter.

We call it the **copycat theory**, and it shows us how people relate to or idolize acts of violence. While most people may watch something tragic on the news in shock or sadness, some people watch the news and think, "You know, I don't feel heard. No one hears me, either. I'm upset. I'm depressed. I'm hopeless. I'm all these different things too, and you know what? If that's the only way that people can hear me, I'm going to pack up my AK-47 and my Glock, and I'm going to walk into that workplace tomorrow, and I'm going to kill as many people as I can, too. Then everyone will hear me like they're hearing this person on TV now."

Why People Identify

Many times, people see some kind of collective identity in a perpetrator or perpetrators of violence. In sci-fi, the Borg from Star Trek are a great example. If you are a Star Trek fan, you will remember this fictional alien race. The Borg are a collection of species that have turned into cybernetic organisms functioning as drones. They operate as a hive and share a collective mind. I believe that many criminals also have this kind of collective identity, a social self, that is part of something bigger than themselves.

It is always good to remember why people identify with perpetrators of violence. Usually, it happens because people are feeling powerless, and violence or the threat of violence makes them feel more powerful or connected to somebody who had this power. When people feel taken advantage of, whether real or imagined, they feel powerless, as if someone else is controlling them. We see early signs of potential copycat violence when we hear things such as, "I could see why someone would kill." "I could see why he did that." "I can understand why they were so upset to go in there with an AK-47." "I can see why he or she killed their partner after the divorce."

Social psychologists have had interest in concepts of identity and individuality since long ago. George Mead focused his theories on the relationship between individual identity and society. The collective identity of a group is often expressed through a group culture or set of traditions. It focuses on the identity of the group as a whole. American gunfights, Malaysian sabotage of combines, and Rwandan massacres do not greatly resemble each other, but they all involve collective violence. There is no individual action but a large array of social interactions. Social unrest such as a riot is the most elementary form of collective violence.

Anger, rage, and violence are all forms of power. They're not a good power, but they're power nonetheless, so we must first watch for the anger phase in people around us before it develops into violence. But we also need to know if something is happening in the world. That means we have to pay closer attention to events happening outside the scope of our day-to-day lives to better prepare ourselves for the chance that those events may seep into our lives unexpectedly.

For example, one of my clients runs a warehouse. Her approach is preventative, not reactive. Anytime something major is happening in the world connected to a terrorist attack or even workplace violence, she calls me.

Usually, when there is an act of violence on the news, especially terrorism, it occurs in properties that are soft targets. A hardened target is one where the security measures are in place, but a soft target is where anyone can walk in and just go *boom*! So clients such as the museum, who are soft targets, want to harden themselves as a potential target during that time. Hardening the target would be increased security in case something happens.

In the warehouse director's case, it's not necessary to increase the security forever, but she recognized what's going on in the world, and she took extra precautions to make sure the facility is safe. It may cost an extra few dollars, but it's worth the peace of mind to know that they have that security during that time.

Identifying a Copycat Threat

"Hey, I just saw this story on the news, and it made me think of a particular employee. We've been having some issues with him. Do you have ten minutes to talk to me about it, Dana? I just want to make sure I'm on track with it."

These are the words of someone who reached out to me in a nondirect way to let me know of an issue they were having in their workplace. Should you ever receive a call like this, or have a thought like this, acknowledge them immediately and thank them for their support and discretion. Let them know you will be following up on their coworker. Letting the staff know that you are open to hearing the good and the bad without repercussions is an invaluable tool.

Clients of mine have heard employees cite things from the news, such as, "You know, the way you treat me, you're lucky I don't drive a truck through here like that guy did in France."

Troubled employees often make a reference to something current because they're angry and want to intimidate you. It could be anything from the San Bernardino shooting to what happened in Paris. The thought is, "You know, that's what I feel like doing," or it may be more explicit, such as, "Careful. That's what I will do." It may just be behavior that is a little odd, but something happened, and it's wise to keep extra eyes on the individual.

Taking these actions helps prevent violence from happening. Instead of looking the other way or being so busy with our lives because we have a project deal, we have to slow ourselves down. If we don't slow ourselves down and deal with these issues, then they're going to get worse. Before we realize there's any trouble, we're in a problem without any solution.

Once I'm called in to assess the threat level, the first thing I notice is whether someone has had a knee-jerk reaction. We've all said things like, "You know, I just want to kill that guy," but it doesn't mean we're going to. But in an assessment, I have to get into the mind of the person in question and feel what they're feeling and see whether or not they mean that and whether they have any intention of doing it. If you're a corporate leader and you see someone in the workplace who seems to identify with a perpetrator of an act of violence, what should you do?

If you have a threat management team on-site, which usually comprises someone from legal, HR, security, and maybe a high-ranking manager, then you need to meet and follow reporting procedures. If that team feels they can't handle the situation because it's something beyond their training, then they should then call someone like me, bring me in, and then we would then look at the situation to see whether it's serious or not.

People can't afford to play practical jokes anymore regarding threats of harm, due to the seriousness that the world looks upon workplace violence and terrorism, especially in an airport. We can't use thoughtless words anymore or make idle threats. This is not the world we live in now.

What Can Be Done!

If you find yourself being confronted by an attacker or catch someone planning an attack, keep the following in mind:

- Don't get involved with whatever situation is going on at the moment. Some people tend to think they can fix it.
- Let the police handle the crisis.
- If you are dealing with a violent person, try to be calm. Don't yell at him or her.
- Run, if you can.

CHAPTER 9

Impulsivity

In my late twenties, while I was still a police officer working the Hollywood division, one of my friends was a fellow officer whom I'll call "Susan." Though I was unaware of it throughout most of our time together on the force, Susan had developed a drinking problem in an effort to battle depression.

As a police officer, Susan had a gun, which with her heavy alcohol consumption was a dangerous combination. She was a good police officer, gentle, caring, loving—she wasn't a heavy-handed type of field cop in any way. She really cared about her job, and she cared about people. I always found her to be one of the good guys, but she had self-esteem issues. Coupled with her alcohol issues and access to guns, this was a trifecta of potential trouble.

At about 2 a.m. one night, I pulled someone over for running a red light in Hollywood and, as I was giving him a ticket, another patrol car pulled up behind me and out stepped Susan, intoxicated.

The challenge with Susan was that she was battling depression, and she self-medicated with alcohol. Quite often, people actually commit suicide as they are beginning to come out of depression. You have to have some energy to take your own life. As strange as it sounds, a person in a deep depression just doesn't have the energy. The time you most need to watch people for suicide risk is as they are coming out of their depression, when they have just enough energy to actually take their own life.

Her depression alone might not have been enough to push her to the edge, but her serotonin levels were already low and were made even lower by her drinking, a chemical effect in the brain caused by alcohol. When you have that combination in someone who is easily able to grab a gun, like Susan, the impulsive act of suicide has an extremely high potential. I don't think that she planned on taking her life that night. I believe that, in that moment, all the right things were in play—alcohol, a service weapon, and coming out of a depression—which all contributed to Susan shooting herself in the head. I believe that that was an impulsive act. While these types of impulsive incidents are incredibly difficult to predict much less prevent, there are some signs to look out for and precautions we can take—all of which I wish I had known more about prior to Susan's death.

Removing the Ability to Act

It is important to note that you should be very aware of the surroundings of whomever you suspect of having the potential to do violence, whether you're scared that they might want to hurt someone else or themselves.

The first question is: What does this person have around them? In most cases, we need to remove weapons. In Susan's case, however, her livelihood required a firearm. Police officers have to have a weapon, so we have the added scrutiny of asking if that person needs to be removed from the field and have their weapon taken away.

Rage and impulsive aggression are different from anger. Anger is a feeling. Rage and impulsive aggression are actions or behaviors, and that's when it really gets scary, whether that be in a domestic violence situation, an act of workplace violence, or any other act of enraged violence.

I once had a client in a domestic violence situation where one partner was sleeping and the enraged partner started to hit her in her sleep, pushing her hard to wake her up and screaming at her. The catalyst was something innocuous. The sleeping person, Betty, had left her Las Vegas hotel room to go to a room next door where her friends were staying, to hang out and watch TV. She sent a text to her partner, Nicole, saying, "Just want to let you know that if you wake up, I'm next door. I'm with Ann and Bill watching TV."

Nicole didn't wake up when the text beeped, so Betty came back to the room, went to bed, and fell asleep. Nicole woke up, read the text, and saw that Betty had left the room to go watch some TV next door while she'd been sleeping. That text, and the implication that she'd been left alone, triggered her to fly from anger into rage in an instant, prompting her to push and hit her partner and scream, "How could you have left me in this room alone?"

This was a secure five-star hotel in Vegas, and Betty was only one room over, but the idea that she'd been left alone scared her and this brought up fear—perhaps she'd been subjected to abuse or abandonment in childhood and the text message was a trigger that led to impulsive action and to strike out at her partner.

Assessing the Threat of Impulsivity

In the 1960s and 1970s, a psychologist named Walter Mischel conducted the Stanford Marshmallow Experiment, which was a study based on delayed gratification. He took a group of children and put them in a room. The proctor would walk in and say, "I'm going to leave the room, and I'm going to come back, it's going to be about fifteen minutes. For those of you who can wait until I get back, you can have two marshmallows. And for those of you who can't wait until I get back, you can have one marshmallow."

This was a test about impulsivity. The study followed those children until their adult years and found that the ones who were able to withhold their impulsivity and wait for the proctor to return had higher SAT scores than those who didn't wait. Mischel also talked to the parents of these children and explained that the ones who were able to avoid acting impulsively tended to be more balanced individuals, as measured by SAT scores, body mass index (BMI), and other life measures.

In 2011, a brain imaging study was conducted on the Stanford participants, which showed there were key differences between those with high delay times and those with low delay times in two areas of the brain by the time they reached mid-life. The brain imaging study showed more-balanced levels in the prefrontal cortex and a more well-balanced brain in the nonimpulsive participants versus the impulsive. When the participants reached mid-life, they were presented with something alluring to tempt them into a response. The study found that participants that delayed or withstood the temptation had a more active prefrontal cortex and the more impulsive participants had a more active ventral striatum (an area linked to addiction). In other words, the kids who were less impulsive tended to be more well-balanced, well-rounded adults than those who were impulsive.

Generally speaking, the more impulsive we are, the more trouble we get into, whether it be violence toward self, toward others, or just impulsivity overall, such as impulsive spending or eating. Whatever it is that you are impulsive about, it never really works out to your advantage.

Impulsive Versus Instrumental Aggression

There are two crucial distinctions in psychology between aggression and violence: impulsive versus instrumental aggression.

Psychologists understand that aggression is a behavior aimed at harming another member. *Impulsive aggression*—often known as irritable, angry, expressive aggression—is marked by strong emotion, especially anger. Anger that turns into a rage is aimed at hurting another person. Instrumental aggression is cooler, and the hurt is delivered in a cold, calculating way.

Psychopaths are an example of more instrumental aggression. They're cold, they control others, and they have no empathy. This is much more calculating than pure anger venting, and we may not always be able to see it coming because the true psychopath can be charming and bright and can hide it more from us. In the Columbine school violence, which we will discuss later, one of those two teenagers is now considered to have been a psychopath. The other was more of a depressed person with impulse control problems. Of course, the psychopath was the one who controlled that entire shooting spree.

Because we know that impulsive aggression is related to low levels of serotonin in the brain, we really want to identify those with depression or substance abuse problems and try to contain what that person has access to, if at all possible.

Identifying Impulse Control Issues in Employees

Unfortunately, the only way we can assess impulsivity is when we have already witnessed acts of impulsivity. If a client calls me in, there has to be a previous incident for me to assess. For example, a forklift driver driving erratically or getting angry and throwing his or her helmet to the ground would qualify as an act of deficient impulse control. I can take that instance and look at the rest of the picture. I can apply my 10-Point Threat Assessment Model to establish whether this is something we can contain.

As a threat assessment expert, with this information I can identify whether the person is a low-, moderate-, or high-risk threat by using actuarial evaluations that specifically talk to anger, impulsivity, and/or alcohol issues. I use that as a guide and again add a little science, experience, research, and intuition to decide the threat level the person poses. There is no foolproof way to decide whether someone is going to be violent, but with this information, I can provide intervention support so that the organization can treat this particular person—if they even want to treat them at all.

If the client does want to work with the employee to find a solution, then the person can be sent for counseling or EAP services. If that person has a drinking or drug problem, then the situation will be worse and makes treatment even more important. The therapist can get a release from the employee to discuss parts of his or her treatment with their employer. Not all information will be available to the employer, however, due to confidentiality requirements. But, generally, anger management should be part of this treatment, meaning we can identify whether impulsivity is being contained.

Anger management therapy itself is changing. It used to include taking a pillow and banging it against a wall. The person would supposedly release their anger and feel better. This goes for children playing with foam noodles for the pool. But later studies disputed this, saying that all it did was beget more violence. Essentially, people need learn to breathe and stop for a minute and say, "Stop!" They need to articulate: "Stop. I'm not going to do this," to contain impulsive actions and anger outbursts.

So how do we know when impulsivity is dangerous or benign? We look at frequency and severity of incidents first. One or two indirect threats or intimidating outbursts would be considered low risk, as would one or two angry outbursts or displays of a hostile style or incidents of perceived harassment. Moderate risk is two or more threats with increasing specificity; for example, conscious intimidation or repeated bullying, angry outbursts, or patterns of harassment. High risk would be clear, direct threats. It would involve repeated fear-inducing boundary crossings, grabbing, grappling, striking, hitting, or slapping. It would include the employee who says things like, "I want to kill everyone. I want to kill Linda at work. Not only do I want to kill Linda, I want to use explosives to the blow the whole place up." Here there are multiple threats and ultimatums, especially toward an authority figure. However, I want to make this very clear; these are all guidelines. It's not to say that a high-risk individual cannot sway from these guidelines; hence a threat assessment is always needed in these types of situations to apply expertise, research, and experience into making a calculated assessment of the risk factor.

How to Contain Impulsivity

If you are a workplace leader, you can contain or reduce the threat of impulsivity in employees by introducing boundaries. You should tell an employee displaying impulse control problems what the boundaries are in very clear and direct terms. For instance, "This is what you can do, and this is what you can't do; this is what I expect from you." It's just like parenting: parents who don't parent their children are going to be in a lot more trouble when that child gets older if they don't introduce boundaries.

Workers want boundaries. They want to feel safe, and they want to know they're doing a good job, but they also need to be told what to do and not to do. Very few people can function autonomously. For some people, boundaries that seem innate to most other people don't exist. They need special guidance, so it's important to counsel them and give them ongoing evaluations. Let them know what they're doing well and not so well. Identify areas of improvement, and let them also know the things that you won't put up with. Importantly, if you see that they start to go out of bounds, you need to call EAP services or a threat assessment expert.

Most people in the workplace don't want to get in someone's personal lives, and they're not supposed to. But, at some point, we must recognize what's going on in someone's personal life because it may flow over into the workplace. If you feel there may be a potential problem, you can say, "As your boss, I'm going to continue to help guide you as well in the work area and help you to feel safe and do the best job that you can. What will make your life easier is if you call this number." It is a good idea to be able to refer them to a service or support group that can help them.

What Can Be Done!

If you have any inkling that an employee could be volatile or impulsive, have a meeting in a room where everything is taken off the desk—pens and pencils, stapler, everything. Position your desk so that you are closer to the door than they are, because if they get angry, they're going to block the door and you're not going to be able to get out.

Managers never think of this. They might ask, "What could be a weapon?" Well, pencils can be a weapon, whether they're blunted or sharpened. Coffee mugs and staplers could be a projectile. A car can be a weapon. Anything can be a weapon if it can hurt you.

You need to anticipate that you may be dealing with someone who can be impulsive at any given moment.

I teach basic safety measures to help people know what to do in situations where there is a risk of an impulsivity issue. It is critical to set boundaries for employees in any situation, but especially for impulsive employees. One solution is drafting a company-wide letter that clearly states the repercussions if employees are caught engaging in certain unacceptable behaviors. Employees should sign this document.

The letter is only one part. Basic safety measures should also be put in place to help all employees recognize when they could be in danger. Train your employees to listen—really listen—to what a distraught coworker is saying. You can't teach them to care, but training your employees to diffuse situations with patience and by setting boundaries can save lives. It's never too early to take precautions and make an action plan for emergencies, and make sure everyone is prepared to escape if there is ever an explosive episode.

CHAPTER 10

The Means and Confidence to Perpetrate Violence

The massacre at Columbine High School in Colorado on April 20, 1999, was a complex and planned attack. The perpetrators, senior students Eric Harris and Dylan Klebold, used ninety-nine explosive devices, car bombs, and a firebomb to divert firefighters. They also converted propane tanks to bombs and placed them in the cafeteria and then shot to death twelve students and one teacher. They injured twenty-four more, three of whom were injured while attempting to escape. The pair subsequently committed suicide.

Harris was especially confident. Harris's journal later showed that he was likely a psychopath. He was well spoken, sweet, and calculating. Klebold, as I mentioned in the last chapter, was more of a depressive type and tended to follow Harris. Harris knew what he wanted to do and even made a final video saying good bye and apologizing to their friends and families. I don't know why mass violence perpetrators like Harris tend to apologize for what they are about to do, but in most cases they do.

The Columbine High School massacre was one year in the planning. These two had the means to do it. They planned, they acquired the firearms, and they knew exactly how they were going to carry out this massacre. They had everything they felt they needed to carry out murder, suicide, arson, and bombings. They wanted to be able to carry it out in the biggest way possible, because they wanted to be known in history for it. It was a clear case of people having the means and confidence to carry out violence.

This is why, during an assessment, it is important to look at means and confidence, because if they don't have both of those things, then it is not going to be able to happen.

Assessing the Means, Confidence, and Intention

The first question I ask in assessing people's means and confidence is, "Do you have guns in the house?" Admittedly, people can lie, but they often like to brag about owning guns. I also ask if they play around with explosives or research how to make pipe bombs online. You'd be surprised at how many people actually tell me the truth. No one has every admitted to me that they wanted to kill anyone, even though they may, but they will admit to their arsenal because they're very proud of it. Some will actually say, "Yeah, I possess explosives. I go on the Internet and I take a look at things." Others might just say, "Yeah, I own a couple of shotguns but just for hunting."

I ask direct questions to determine their means, such as, "How confident are you with the gun? Do you go shooting? When was the last time you went shooting? Do you hunt? Do you have a hunter's license?" While they are talking, I try to probe into their psyche in regard to confidence level.

Somebody might say, "Yeah, I live with my dad. He has a shotgun, but I never even picked it up. I wouldn't even know what to do with it." Nevertheless, I'll still get a feeling for where they are in terms of their confidence level with either weapons of mass destruction, bombs, shotguns, side arms, or some other type of weaponry. Often, it is in the silence between direct questions, when they don't say anything, that I get a feeling for potential issues.

If you're a workplace leader, then you need to make sure that the person asking the questions is not afraid to ask direct questions. They may need to ask, "Do you want to kill yourself? Do you want to kill somebody else? Have you ever thought of homicide? How many guns do you own?" Again, these are all very important questions. This should be done by a threat assessment expert.

You should also ask what type of magazines they like to read or what type of TV shows they like to watch. Just because their reading material or TV preferences are violent doesn't mean they're potentially violent, but it is part of the puzzle when assessing your situation. You need to assess their state of mind and you can do that with multiple direct questions.

Other elements to note include whether the subject has shown any inappropriate interest in mass violence or terrorism. Has the person engaged in any type of attack-related behaviors, developed an attack idea or plan, or even thought about a plan? They may not think they'll actually follow through if they have, but it's important to ask hypothetical questions, such as, "Have you ever thought about what you would do if you did want to harm someone?"

Using Empathy

When I am called in to assess a person's potential for an act of mass violence, I always want to set a welcoming and accepting tone with the individual first. I begin by empathizing with them, expressing that I know they don't really want to hurt someone, but I will still ask if they've ever thought about it because they're upset. I'll then ask what that plan would look like. This is a way to try to get them to open up to me, to understand what their thought process or behavioral patterns look like. I'll also assess potential triggers, such has whether there have been any recent failures in their life, a bad performance appraisal, or some kind of loss or bankruptcy. In other words, I want to know what the stressful events in their lives are.

If someone is too depressed, then I'm less concerned about them having the means or confidence to perpetrate violence. If they're in a deep state of depression, then I know I have some time working on my side, and I take advantage of that. But if they're coming out of that depression and have a bit more energy, then I know I have less time to figure out what's going on with them and develop a containment plan.

If a potential threat exists, then I implement plans to inform the situation. One option is to implement surveillance to gather the information I need. I want to know if they are going to the gun store. I want to know what their house looks like. Are they keeping it up, mowing the lawn? I'll have a surveillance operative drive by and take a look at their car to tell me what it looks like. Is it clean or dirty, are there cigarette butts and newspapers everywhere? Or is it clean and tidy? This helps get into the person's mind-set to assess what they may or may not do.

Another tactic that will help me understand them better is talking to the supervisors or any of their coworkers, although this requires care because of confidentiality issues. I don't want things to get out. Sometimes, the only option I have is talking only to the suspicious person and reading personnel records to see whether they feel confident enough to carry out any type of violence.

Proximity Concerns

Proximity is a factor in making a threat assessment. The further away from the workplace potential threats are, the better I feel. If they live far away from the facility, then they're going to have to really want to do something to get in that car and drive a long distance to deliver some type of violence. If someone has been terminated and they live fifty miles away, returning to inflict violence takes a lot more effort. People don't drive that far unless they're absolutely focused and determined.

However, if they're nearby, there is greater concern. They may come back to case the place. Maybe they just want to show their presence, show that they're there, and then leave. Nevertheless, that has potential to elevate. Most likely they are moving toward violence because they can't let this thing go and they are close enough to act on it at any given moment.

Another proximity issue relates to face-to-face arguments. We see this among high-functioning people: when people get angry with someone, they tend to move closer to the person. We may not even be conscious of it, but we want to overpower that individual. It makes us feel bigger than life.

If you are on the receiving end of this action, the best response is to back up and turn your body to a forty-five-degree angle and open up that space between you and the angry person to defuse the anger. This will work for anger but not rage. Rage is something totally different, but when you are dealing with anger, this movement can help to defuse that situation.

Removing Destabilizers

When it comes to proximity to destabilizers—such as weapons, drugs, alcohol—threat assessment experts, security, or law enforcement want to remove these items from that person's proximity to decrease the chance of that kind of impulsive act or that immediate means to have access to something. For example, with Susan, if that gun hadn't been there, she could have taken a bottle of pills. But often, when someone takes a bottle of pills, they can change their mind. They can pick up the phone to call a friend or an ambulance. They may reach out for help. But once they pull that trigger, there's no going back.

As a threat assessment expert, my recourse with people who have the potential to harm themselves or others is to remove the firearms from the house. I will put them in a safe if possible. In one case I worked on, the woman involved lived with her father who had guns in the house, so I asked him to either buy a safe that she didn't have the combination to or take the guns out of the house and put them someplace else. He locked them up.

In another case involving a couple, I had the higher-functioning partner take all the guns—four or five rifles and handguns—to his father's house.

Removing destabilizers isn't going to prevent someone from going out to buy a gun, but we can remove the close proximity factor and watch for more signs of escalation. With the Columbine incident, if people had paid more attention and had seen what was happening, and had paid more attention to the clear signs that there was a problem, I believe that situation could have been contained.

Signs of Means and Confidence

As a corporate leader, it's important to notice the signs or signals that somebody has the confidence to do violence. You need to intuitively think about whether you may have an issue. Signs can include increased absenteeism, increased tardiness, and/or lack of concentration. Perhaps your suspect is always alone, doesn't say a lot, doesn't socialize, doesn't have smoke breaks with the others, or doesn't go out for lunch.

I was called in on a case once involving a person who kept to themselves and never talked to anyone. One day he walked into the Xerox room and said, out of the blue, to another employee, "You know, I really wish I could just blow this place up." Then he walked out of the room. Two minutes later, he walked back in and added, "You know, I'm really serious. I'm really serious. I am so frustrated. I just hate this place." He walked out again.

The person doing the Xeroxing reported the incident to the manager, who called the corporate security director, who called me. Because they were in a different state, I arranged for a plainclothes, off-duty cop to be there within two hours to make sure everything was okay. Then I got on the phone with the man in question and started talking to him about his comments and my concerns. It turned out he was just frustrated; I assessed him as a low/moderate risk. Next, I went to the corporate leader and talked about actions the company could take to make that employee feel better about himself, such as reaching out to him, setting boundaries, interacting with him, and giving him some guidance.

Once they did that, he actually became a much better worker. It ended up working out okay instead of disastrously.

What Can Be Done!

If you think you have an employee who could be violent, it will likely be too dangerous and involve too much responsibility to confront that person alone. It's best to call a threat assessment expert in to sit down with the person and make a complete assessment.

> What to do if you suspect an employee has the means and confidence to act violently:
>
> - Call the police and give detailed information.
> - Don't get involved.
> - If you have to deal with a violent person talk calmly whatever you do don't yell at the person
> - Understand that this person may have lost touch with common shared human reality

CHAPTER 11

Neurological Disorders and Aggression

Quite often, clinicians or threat assessment experts will overlook the issue of neurological disorders and aggression. It can sometimes be misunderstood as a mental illness or substance abuse issue, but the chance that there could be a neurological dysfunction behind a person's suspicious behavior should not be discounted. There could be a brain tumor leading to a propensity toward violence, for instance. It's rare, but it can happen.

Typically, what happens when a corporate leader has suspicions about an employee is he or she will call me and ask for a fitness-for-duty exam. As we've discussed before, this is basically a psychological exam or threat assessment to see whether this person is a threat to self or others, or whether they can return to work.

However, what many clinicians and the workplace overlook is a medical exam, which is just as critical as a psychological exam because aggression can result from medical, neurological, or psychiatric disorders. An MRI or a CAT scan can provide more information, but they're expensive. The tendency, therefore, is to send the employee for a fitness-for-duty test, conduct an interview, and possibly do some psych tests, such as an actuarial test. There is an abundance of these available online for multiple disciplines. Testing people to see how they can succeed with their given skill set can be fulfilling to the employee as much as it is helpful to you as an employer.

In addition to testing, there needs to be an interview, and this interview needs to ask the right questions.

Recently, I did an assessment of a Hispanic man, Carlos Ramirez, because he had made comments that concerned his employer. Carlos said, "There are going to be casualties." People immediately thought he was threatening to become violent. But this isn't necessarily so, which is why it's important to probe further into what people tell you. In this case, his intended meaning was that more people were going to quit the job. "More people are going to resign," he told me in an interview. "If we're not managed right and we're not given respect, more of us are not going to want to work here."

Meanwhile, the company leader and employees expected him to come to work with a gun and hurt them, when all he was saying was that the company was dysfunctional, not that he wanted to kill people. Nevertheless, he was gay and Hispanic, and more to the point, had once attempted suicide, so I asked him, "What do you think about what happened at Pulse in Florida? How did that make you feel?"

He didn't pause, which meant he didn't think. He gave me a spontaneous answer, which I like. "It was horrible. It was horrific," he said. "The first thing I did was get with my other friends. We wanted to talk to the press about how this is not what minorities are about. We're not about violence. We don't condone this."

This is why it's important to ask the right questions. I'm not a psychiatrist or a neurologist, but I am informed enough to know when to identify suspicious behavior and know when to send someone to a neurologist to see if there's anything else going on besides a psychiatric disorder. If I suspect someone has the potential be violent, then I might recommend this path to the organization, but it's up to the corporate leader to go through with it.

I rated Carlos a low risk for violence toward others but low to moderate risk for the self-infliction of harm, such as suicidal ideations. He had attempted suicide in his twenties, and although he was in his forties when I interviewed him, I was nevertheless cautious of a small but measurable risk based on past behavior.

I told him I was concerned but that there were things that made me feel better about his situation. He was part of a men's support group, he had friends, and he had family members to support him. He saw a psychiatrist every few months for medication and weekly therapy. Had he seen the psychiatrist only to get meds every few months and neglected therapy, I would have been concerned. Essentially, he had a lot of elements in place to help contain any type of self-damage that he may want to do to himself.

Had I felt he posed more of a threat, I would have referred him for a medical exam. I would have asked him if he had headaches, where, and how often, and whether he ever felt dizzy or nauseous. In other cases, where the person responded affirmatively to these questions, I recommended sending him out for a medical and not just doing a threat assessment.

Awareness

Corporate leaders and fellow workers need to start being aware of their surroundings and be less self-absorbed. We often overlook putting ourselves and other people in dangerous situations. For example, I was called in to assess a young man, Brian, a high-functioning, smart sixteen-year-old kid who lived with his mother, a ten-year old sibling, and the mother's husband. The mother had her own self-esteem issues and was probably in a very dysfunctional relationship with her husband. In this case, the dysfunction was with the entire family unit.

One day, she took both children to the home of her father-in-law, who suffers from dementia. There are patients with dementia who present with aggression and agitation, and this particular man had a tendency to act out aggressively.

That day, he started to become aggressive with the mother and pushed her up against a wall. The kids ran away. She hid behind a door, but her father-in-law was trying to get to her by pushing the door open. She was screaming for help. Brian came running in, thinking his mother was in harm's way, grabbed his pocketknife, and stabbed the old man, who later died.

Brian was arrested and held at juvenile hall for a month. The district attorney was after a murder conviction. To get this conviction, they needed to look at the level of force used. Was it necessary? Could Brian have intimidated the old man? Could he have just pushed him away? What else could the young man have done to a seventy-year-old with dementia?

If we back up, we can ask the sort of questions that should have been asked at the outset. Why put Brian in a home with an older man with dementia who displays aggressive behavior? We need to think about the choices we make. We need to take responsibility for putting an employee, who is maybe not the highest functioning person but who does his job, with a manager who is too assertive, too aggressive, lacks empathy, and lacks respect. Don't you think this will have a bad outcome?

By lacking awareness of our environment and the people in it, we fail to take responsibility for the acts of violence that other people do. This does not justify their behavior, but we need to be much more aware of our contribution to the pressure situation in which we put them.

For Further Reading about Neurological Disorders and Chemical Imbalances

Murderous Minds by Dean A. Haycock, Ph.D.

Biology and Violence from Birth to Adulthood by Deborah W. Denno

Violent Behavior and Mental Illness by Carl C. Bell

Aggression and Psychosis

Too often, we believe that aggression is linked to psychosis or to substance abuse. We focus on brain imaging tests, neuropsychological testing, and EEGs to see what might be forming in the individual's brain chemistry, but we rarely think aggression can happen due to a neurological disorder.

Lithium is often used to subdue an individual and to deter chronic aggressive behavior. But there are drawbacks to lithium, such as shaking hands, tremors, and nausea, which is why a lot of patients don't want to take certain psychotropic medications. If they go off the medication, the aggressiveness starts again. It's like a never-ending circle of misery for people with these neurological disorders. They are torn between aggressive behavior and feeling ill.

Research is becoming more precise in identifying and finding treatments for the abnormalities of the brain. In this work, it's important because these can underlie violence and aggression. New findings can be used to help clinicians diagnose children and adolescents with different types of behavioral problems to treat them more effectively. However, we need more research to get a better handle on the neurological roots of aggression.

Identifying Potential Neurological Disorders in an Employee

If an employee has a possible neurological disorder, you will likely first notice that the person is a loner. They're isolated. They may throw things or behave impulsively. They may not take care of safety issues, such as not wearing their helmet when they're riding a forklift or not wearing their gloves if they're welding. Something should bring your attention to that person.

The next step in tackling this problem is to call on your internal threat assessment team, and if they can't handle it, then call in a threat assessment expert. The expert should not only go through a threat assessment or a fitness-for-duty test, but should also send the person out for a neurological test or a general medical test at the very least to see if there's anything medically going on with them that may be causing the aggression.

Being aware of a potential threat in your company and then doing nothing makes the company liable. If you do something, make sure you document everything, even just calling the police and asking for an extra patrol. They police may run a background check, since they can access more information than can a private individual. These simple steps are doing something in terms of corporate liability.

The next step is conducting a threat assessment. Remember, if the threat assessment expert puts something in writing as far as recommendation to contain the threat and you don't follow through with those recommendations and a violent event occurs, you may have liability. The threat assessment report becomes a legal report and can be subpoenaed. If you don't want to run that risk, or want to consider whether to implement the recommendations or not, then ask for verbal recommendations.

What Can Be Done!

If you suspect someone in your office has a neurological disorder:

- Contact your internal threat assessment team, whether that be HR and/or legal.
- Follow through on your team's recommendations.
- Reach out to a health care or mental health professional who has expertise in assessing threats.
- Call in a threat assessor, but make sure they are or have with them a licensed psychologist or psychotherapist who is trained and experienced in conducting threat assessments.
- Do not confront the employee yourself.

Remember that you are the first line of defense in this scenario, and following proper protocols can help you feel confident that you are not only protecting the workplace but also protecting yourself against any legal issues. Being confident is part of being hopeful, and hope is the driving factor in all aspects of a healthy life. While we can be mindful and appreciate what we already have, having a hope for an even better tomorrow helps people get up every day with a purpose.

CONCLUSION

Hope as a Purpose

> "Hope is a thing with feathers that perches in the soul and sings the tune without the words and never stops at all."
>
> —EMILY DICKINSON

Most of the violence in the world is fear driven, which empowers terrorists, bullies, and any other person of ill will. Our fear allows them to control us, which only further encourages them. The more we retreat out of fear, the more we lose the battle. What is the cure?

Hope. Hope is the antidote for fear.

When I talk about hope, I'm not talking about blind faith. There's a difference between hope and wishing. We want to be hopeful, but we also want to be grounded and realistic; it means actively trying to investigate the best path of action. We don't want to just wishfully think that everything is going to be okay. There's no point thinking, "Everything's going to be fine. I don't have to do anything because I'm just going to wish it to be good." Our hope has to be grounded in some type of reality.

Managers have to really listen, and watch for possible situations. If they are aware of employees who have made threatening comments in the workplace, they can't ignore it and expect things to get better. "I never imagined the employee would actually carry out the threat" is not an excuse. The manager knows the employees, works with them every day, and has seen them at company parties. Hoping things will work out for troubled employees is natural and commendable but only if you have taken the time to establish safety measures and action steps for everyone's protection. At some point, though, we need to have some realistic understanding of actual action items. Hope can carry us through, but there must be some action behind it. This two-part approach is grounded in reality and is vital that we all understand.

Violence does not come out of nowhere, and so we need to look at the source. That's hard to do because, again, it requires us to look at ourselves. Whether it's an act of terrorism or a domestic argument, the normal response is to place blame outward instead of looking inward. It's much harder to look at ourselves and take some responsibility for our part. Did I take part in what caused that employee to throw the stapler at me? Did I say something? Did I emotionally push him or her? It *never* makes it right to use emotional or physical abuse, but we still need to explore if we had a part in disrespecting the person. If this person has no coping skills or boundaries then we are playing with fire. As long as we give respect, we are in a better place to defuse anger and rage from someone who only knows how to blame and act out negatively. Just to be clear, there is nothing anyone can say or do that should put themselves in a position of receiving any kind of abuse. What I am saying is we need to treat people with respect.

The bombing in New York City's Chelsea neighborhood in 2016 showed people's resilience and respect for one another as they responded to terrorism. People got up and went to work. They walked down the street and got a cup of coffee. It didn't stop their day. They were hopeful because they were saying, "Hey, I have hope. I'm going to get up and I'm going to go to work and they're not going to stop me."

When fear keeps us from getting up and doing our thing every day, when fear says, "I'm not going to get up and go to work tomorrow because I'm scared," that is when fear wins.

We need to start getting to the roots of why we have rage and violence and why we are reactive rather than proactive. We could contain a lot of the violence that happens in the world, but first we have to start caring.

The 2017 Las Vegas Strip shooting is currently the deadliest mass shooting in the United States committed by an individual since the June 12 Orlando nightclub shooting a year prior. Fifty-eight people were killed, 450 were wounded, and the lives of many were brutalized in the wake of this tragedy. He used modified weaponry and planned for weeks in advance to inflict as much damage and terror as possible. Similarly, the bombing at the Manchester arena is the second worst terrorist attack in Britain's history after the July 7 London bombings more than a decade prior. The bomb was designed to maim with shrapnel, and therefore it required more than rudimentary knowledge to build than just one young, homegrown attacker. With government facilities intensifying their vigilance, public venues have become the new targets. With these types of attacks on the rise, it is critical that facilities develop exit routes for people in an emergency situation.

The aftermath of both tragedies is a strong example of a community's capacity for compassion. Journalists captured images and stories of officers holding victims, or strangers driving truckloads of injured people to hospitals, and going back to help save more. Perseverance and the human spirit in the United States and in England are stronger than ever before. Like New York and Boston before it, Las Vegas and Manchester showed terrorism will only strengthen their resolve and community against such cowardly acts of violence. There is hope in these tragedies, from a person shielding their loved ones, to others guiding dozens of people to safety in the chaos. Look for the hope. As we start caring more and more, we need to continue to think critically. We don't want to be naïve, nor do we want to make more poor choices. Violence is about controlling others, and the more we retreat from it or blindly fight it, the more we lose. To win, we must examine the violence, searching for why it exists, where it comes from, and how to prevent it. In order to do that, we must come together as people under the hope that we can solve problems without violence. We must start bonding more. We must be more accepting. Hope can't just be individuals hoping. We must come together and devise a plan, in our homes, in our workplaces, in our communities, and in our collective general society.

In the workplace, corporations must push people to be kinder and more accepting of one another. Let's be honest, by nature, we're not always the kindest creatures on the planet. We can be cruel and self-absorbed. We need to come out of our own little cocoons and work to be more altruistic. Humanity has been asking the question repeatedly whether humans are good or bad. For thousands of years philosophers have debated whether we have a basically good nature that is corrupted by society or a basically bad nature that is kept in check by society. This chapter won't be delving into this topic, but this author believes humans are basically good. With that said there is still too much evil lurking in the shadows, too many people lost in a downward spiral, and all of this creates violence.

Whatever it is that you do, you can start by doing something kind for others. If you don't have the financial means, then maybe you can donate a little of your time to helping others in need.

When Carlos, the gay Hispanic man I spoke about in chapter 11, was being held at the hospital on a seventy-two-hour 5150 welfare call, he told me that he would walk up to the other patients and find something whole and beautiful about them.

"Hey, Emily, I really like that sweater," he said to one.

"Really, you do?" she responded.

"Yeah, you look really good, really pretty," he said.

When I asked him why he did that, he responded, "Because I don't want to be self-absorbed. I have serious issues. I know that. But as I give to other people, I help myself."

We are so busy with the stress in our own lives that we sometimes forget to take a moment to see if someone else may be a threat or a risk or is hurting or in pain. We don't stop and consider what we can do to reach out to that person. We forget that we have personal responsibility, that we can choose to be compassionate and hopeful, or that we can choose to be self-absorbed and fearful.

We must remember that we can only allow either hope or fear into our mindset at a given time, which means we must consciously choose one. Choose hope. Choose to acknowledge that hope requires action, and in our hopeful actions, we can conquer fear. It just may save our lives.

APPENDIX

Investigation after Workplace Violence

Here is an abbreviated sample of a checklist by the person completing the report. When assessing an individual, a similar checklist may be used.

INVESTIGATOR: ______________________ DATE: ___________

DATE OF SUSPENSION AND/OR TERMINATION: __________

FULL NAME OF SUBJECT: ____________________________

DATE OF BIRTH: _____ AGE: _____ SS#: __________ SEX: ____

CURRENT HOME ADDRESS: ____________________________

PRIOR ADDRESS: ______________________________________

OTHER KNOWN ADDRESSES (Relatives):

____

KNOWN ASSOCIATES (Relatives, Emergency Contacts, etc.):

____

DATE OF HIRE: __________ OCCUPATION: ________________

ETHNIC BACKGROUND: ________________________________

MARITAL STATUS: ___________________________________

OF CHILDREN AND/OR DEPENDANTS: ________________

WITNESS RESPONSES

NAME: ____

POSITION IN THE ORGANIZATION: ____________________

DATE OF HIRE: _____________________________________

KNOWN SUBJECT FOR: ________________________________

RELATIONSHIP TO SUBJECT: __________________________

1. Does the subject own weapons? Do you know what his/her expertise is with firearms?

2. Does the subject use any type of drug, even prescription drugs? Does he/she drink and how often?

3. Does the subject seek any type of therapy? Any history of a psychological diagnosis? How does he/she deal with stress?

4. Has the subject been involved with the police, either minor or major, even traffic accidents? Are there any DUIs that you are aware of?

5. Is the subject involved in a relationship? If so, with who and for how long? Any knowledge of an affair either presently or in the past?

6. Any idea of the subject's financial well-being? Who does he/she live with?

7. Regarding impulse control, how does the subject deal with confrontation from others? Examples:

8. What religion does the subject practice? Does he/she seem to look at life from an extreme point of view? Examples:

9. Have there been any changes in the subject's mood or behavior over the last year, months, or weeks? Examples:

10. What does the subject do from day to day at work? Are there any commendable or need-to-be-improved work ethics?

Describe this subject's typical day at work. Examples: arrival/departure times, consistent habits or behaviors, inappropriate behaviors, appropriate and/or exemplary behavior.